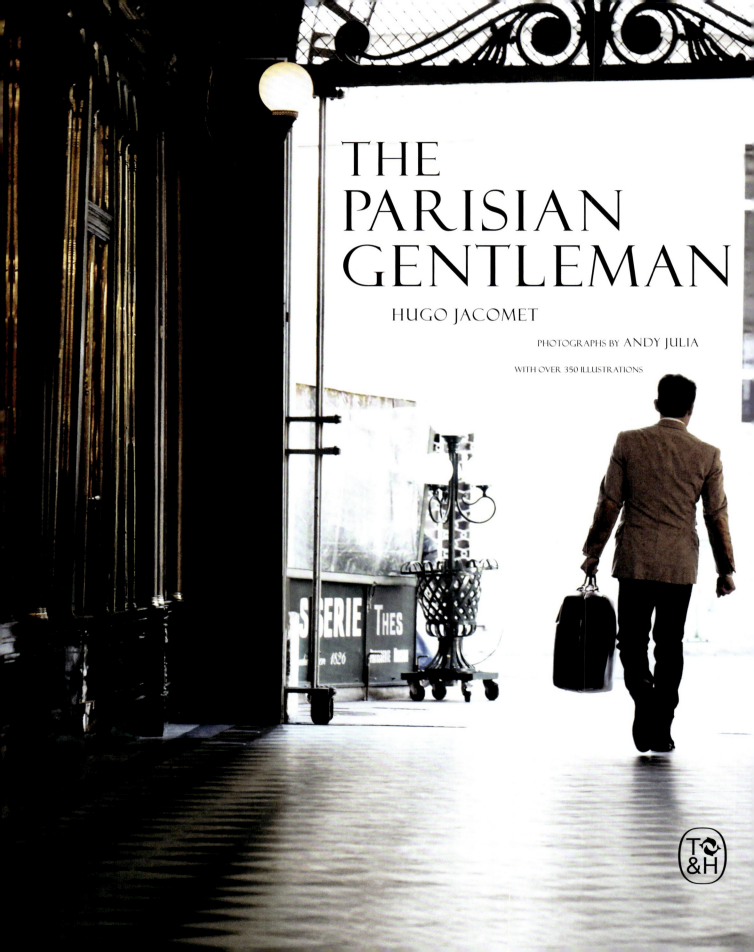

THE
PARISIAN
GENTLEMAN

HUGO JACOMET

PHOTOGRAPHS BY ANDY JULIA

WITH OVER 350 ILLUSTRATIONS

T&H

CONTENTS

First published in the United Kingdom
in 2015 by Thames & Hudson Ltd,
181A High Holborn, London WC1V 7QX

First published in the United States of America in
2018 by Thames & Hudson Inc., 500 Fifth Avenue,
New York, New York 10110

This compact edition first published in 2018
Reprinted 2022

British Library Cataloguing-in-Publication Data
A catalogue record for this book is available
from the British Library

Library of Congress Control Number
2018934140

ISBN 978-0-500-29396-6

Printed and bound in China by
C & C Offset Printing Co. Ltd

MIX
Paper from
responsible sources
FSC
www.fsc.org   FSC® C008047

Be the first to know about our
new releases, exclusive content
and author events by visiting
thamesandhudson.com
thamesandhudsonusa.com
thamesandhudson.com.au

HUGO JACOMET, 'The
Parisian Gentleman', is a lecturer,
curator, author and pioneer of the
menswear revival that celebrates
well-crafted clothing and elegant
gentlemen. Monsieur Jacomet has
a strong following and his digital
magazine, *Parisian Gentleman*,
is a worldwide reference for
sartorial updates and education.

ANDY JULIA is a freelance
photographer based in Paris.

Cover:

Photographs © Andy Julia.
(Front, clockwise from
top left) see pages 82, 53,
226–27, 99; (back) 70–71.

Page 1

A Parisian casual outfit:
bespoke jacket, cardigan
and shirt by Cifonelli;
travel bag Pauline by
Moynat; Big Pilot watch
by IWC.

Pages 2–3

One of Paris's typical
passages. The gentleman
is holding a Paradis bag
by Moynat.

Pages 4–5

Francesco Smalto's bespoke
salon in Paris, with a
portrait of the founder
on the right-hand wall.

These pages

Ready-to-wear shoes
by Berluti.

Foreword by
JAMES SHERWOOD

As Hugo Jacomet writes in the introduction to this handsome, erudite volume, 'this book is here to right a wrong'. He rightly surmises that Parisian haute couture has cast a long shadow over the French capital's formidable history as a home to makers of exceptional bespoke suits and gentlemen's requisites. Received wisdom has it that Paris leads the world in dressing the female of the species, and London's Savile Row the male. Paris could not ask for a more dashing *chevalier* than M. Jacomet to defend the honour of such national treasures as Charvet, Moynat, Berluti and Guerlain, who for generations have proved that the language of male sartorial elegance is not exclusively English.

Although the French Revolution of 1789 was undeniably a gift to London's master tailors, it is a myth that Savile Row is somehow still engaged in a Napoleonic War with Paris and Naples to claim the crown as the world's finest cutters of cloth. There is, was and always will be an *entente cordiale* between the master craftsmen of Paris and London, and an understanding that a parochial attitude is anathema to men who take pride in their manner and mode of dress. I heartily applaud a chap who remains largely faithful to his tailor, but would defy any man 'of the cloth' not to be seduced by the discreet charm of a Cifonelli shoulder line, a Cartier gem-set cufflink or a Simonnot-Godard monogrammed linen handkerchief.

The French gentleman's philosophy of dress is distinctive from the English aristocrat's affected carelessness and the swaggering *sprezzatura* of Italy's peacock males. An English m'lud will draw attention to the frayed cuffs of his Turnbull & Asser shirts as to a badge of honour and boast that his John Lobb oxfords are older than his children. At the other extreme of the sartorial scale, an Italian who isn't as pristine as the promenade in Porto Ercole is beyond contempt. I am in awe of the Parisian male's appreciation for refinement. His taste is studied and acquired rather than inherited; his style walks the line between tradition and flamboyance.

For me, the epitome of Gallic style is the legendary couturier Hubert de Givenchy, whose elegance of mind and generosity of character were and are reflected in his quiet, correct and precise mode of dress, which never overshadows the lady in his company or on his arm. I think of that famous photograph of Givenchy and his muse Audrey Hepburn walking along the Left Bank of the Seine arm in arm, lost in their own company, not dressed to attract eyes or approbation and yet for me a couple who defined the word chic.

What of the man who has made a study of the Parisian gentleman, then? I was introduced to Hugo virtually, via his online *Parisian Gentleman* journal, and discovered a kindred spirit who spoke with equal passion about the unique, idiosyncratic, often family-owned marques that hold fast the floodgates against the global brands that are cloning the world's capital cities. Hugo is a fearless advocate of *maisons* that have earned his respect, and his readers, in turn, respect his advice and judgment. He has a finely tuned antenna for mendacity and is not afraid of speaking his mind, even when he is tweaking the noses of big brands.

When I first met Hugo, in London, I was mesmerized by this apparition who seemed to me

'When an old man dies, a library burns'

Old African proverb

an echo of the Parisian dandy the Count d'Orsay. He is an imposing character and a practised flâneur, as many a cocktail and cigarette shared at (or outside) Cecconi's have admirably demonstrated. But observing Hugo in the workrooms of the Savile Row tailors, it was fascinating to see how swiftly he got to the heart of the craft and held the attention of even the most irascible tailor or cutter. Hugo is an unashamed bon viveur, but he is also a grafter.

In the years I have known Hugo he has proved to be nothing less than a highly skilled diplomat, who has a talent for bringing people of like minds together. When I wrote my first book for Thames & Hudson, *Savile Row: The Master Tailors of British Bespoke*, it was Hugo who organized the Paris launch party, at Old England. Similarly, it was he who co-hosted the Paris reception for my third T&H book, *The Perfect Gentleman: The Pursuit of Timeless Elegance in London*, at Ralph Lauren's town house on boulevard Saint-Germain.

The Parisian Gentleman not only walks in the footsteps of giant style icons, but also shares the secrets of such ateliers as Maison Bonnet, who framed the faces of Yves Saint Laurent, Le Corbusier and I. M. Pei; Guerlain, court perfumer to Emperor Napoleon III and his Empress Eugenie; the Duke of Windsor's shoemaker of choice, Berluti; and Charvet, whose shirts, ties and silk pyjamas graced the wardrobes of King Edward VII, Marcel Proust, Claude Monet, Oscar Wilde, Serge Diaghilev, Fred Astaire, Cecil Beaton, Jean Cocteau and John F. Kennedy, to name a very few.

Although I am a great believer that it is wise to look back before moving forwards, what I appreciate most about *The Parisian Gentleman* is Hugo's refusal to indulge in nostalgia. This book is not a remembrance of things past or an elegy for dying trades. Hugo's words and Andy Julia's principal photography celebrate a renaissance in the Parisian bespoke trade, with ateliers reporting a rise of as much as 30 per cent year on year in the demand for unique, hand-crafted pieces. Hugo may support the independent *maisons*, such as Camps de Luca, Simonnot-Godard and Francesco Smalto, but he is pragmatic in acknowledging that without the investment of LVMH the jewels in its portfolio, such as Moynat, Berluti and Louis Vuitton, would not have the resources to train apprentices and expand the business to meet demand.

As the African proverb says, 'when an old man dies, a library burns'. Thanks in part to the relentless passion and publicity Hugo Jacomet directs towards the fruits of their labours, Parisian master shoe-, shirt- and suit-makers now have a new generation of fledgling dandies at their doors. It is also Hugo's compliment that talented ladies and gentlemen who would perhaps have chosen a career in fashion are instead turning towards the bespoke business, where masters have passed on the arcana of their craft for centuries past and, it is to be hoped, will do so for centuries to come.

James Sherwood

Foreword by
G. BRUCE BOYER

As an avid follower of Hugo Jacomet's online magazine *Parisian Gentleman* since its inception in 2009, I'm delighted that he has collected his thoughts on cosmopolitan French style in this beautiful book. He is, after all, the authority on the subject: not only on its sartorial aspects, but also on all those facets of the luxury life of the gentleman who wishes to be accoutred with distinction in Paris.

First as a fan and then as a friend, I have found that Hugo brings together several talents I admire in a writer. He is at the same time erudite; eminently intelligible, insightful and witty; balanced in his perspective; and thorough in his research. In an online world where anyone can publish anything and it is not always easy to distinguish the men from the boys, Hugo is indeed an expert. His online magazine has served as a school of higher education and a guiding light to the world of the Parisian gentleman.

Hugo has these abilities because he is an incisively stylish gentleman himself, and one who has a great love for his subject, those *maisons* of artisans who have devoted their lives to personal items of handmade quality. Anyone who can talk with authority, philosophical depth and technical detail about the quality of a voile handkerchief or the finesse of tailoring a shoulder one minute, and the sociological implications of nonchalance in dress the next, is well worth reading.

Wedged as it is between the male bastions of London and Naples, Paris is usually perceived, in fashion terms, as a women's world. That beautiful city of lights has been home to exciting haute couture for so long that we forget it is also a formidable city with a long history of luxury for the gentleman. The great *chemisiers*, to name but a small section, are unsurpassed for fine shirts and neckwear. And then there is the famous 'Cifonelli shoulder' so prized by aficionados of bespoke tailoring, and the secret technique of patinating leather used by Berluti in crafting its benchmade shoes.

The *Parisian Gentleman* website has been instrumental in introducing thousands of men around the world to the niceties and finer points of Gallic style, those objects of desire from handcrafted shoes to cologne and stationery. Each time Hugo tackles a subject, whether it be buying lisle hosiery or how to recognize the cut of a pristine Francesco Smalto suit, you can be sure that he will frame it within the zeitgeist and relate it to our lives in a useful and accessible way. Decidedly aspirational, to say the least.

All the *addresses d'or*, those renowned Parisian shops and ateliers of glowing heritage, are described here with the loving attention they so richly deserve. One might say that craftsmanship is the real theme of this handsome book. As technology rushes us into a future we cannot imagine, artisanal work becomes a refuge, a place of rest and refreshment. The artistry and beauty of craftsmanship are alive and well in Paris: Cifonelli, Camps de Luca and Smalto, Charvet and Vuitton, Guerlain, Cartier, Simonnot-Godard, Berluti and Corthay are some of the names of legend and dreams that are thoroughly and illuminatingly discussed here.

The Parisian Gentleman is a poem to artisans, and Hugo Jacomet is the consummate guide to the Parisian makers of distinction for the gentleman, precisely because he is one himself. We can all learn more than a thing or two from him.

G Bruce Boyer

A detail of Camps de Luca's bespoke salon in Paris, looking on to the famous place de la Madeleine. This is now a historical picture: in March 2015, after forty-five years in this salon, Camps de Luca moved to the no less famous rue de la Paix.

PREFACE

During a sleepless night in January 2009, my life changed completely.

It must have been 3 or 4 am. To tell the truth, I could probably use software to find the very minute when it all happened. But although this was a turning point in my life, I still prefer to think back on it with the blurred charm of reminiscence and the patina of human memory.

My name is Hugo Jacomet. I am the grandson of Maxime Jacomet, a shoemaker and cobbler in the Deux-Sèvres, a rural area in the west of France, and the son of Janick Jacomet, a seamstress in Paris.

When I was growing up, whenever my parents bought me new shoes I would always refuse to wear them for the first few days. I didn't want to soil the squeaky-clean soles of those leathery objects whose texture, smell, impeccable seams and pristine uppers fascinated me. They were more than practical items for walking. I confess without shame that I sometimes even slept with them on.

Forty years later, although I still have trouble inflicting on my shoes the terrible trauma of that first step on to the tarmac of the streets, I can account very well for that mild obsessiveness that made three generations of my family laugh. I have spent the last ten years of my life studying, investigating, scrutinizing, analysing and commenting on the wonderful world of master tailors and bootmakers throughout the world. I am therefore now able to appreciate fully the incredible amount of skill, work, passion, strenuous effort, complexity, craftsmanship and even love that goes into the making of a bespoke pair of shoes or a suit made according to the gospel of traditional tailoring.

Just to keep busy on that wakeful night in January 2009, I decided to compose a text on men's style, a topic close to my heart and one that struck me as full of untold things to write about and share. In just a few clicks I created a blog using a free provider that pressurized me into choosing a name I wouldn't be able to change later. The name *Parisian Gentleman* was an instinctive choice, and I couldn't imagine that my readers would soon equate the phrase with me as a person. I published my very first text immediately – just a short piece; nothing extraordinary. It was a brief message that even my most dedicated readers do not remember today.

After shutting down my laptop I eventually went to sleep, thinking that I would read the piece again in the morning and most likely erase it. After all, I am an expert in communications and I know that nightly thoughts and, to an even greater degree, texts rarely sound relevant when breakfast comes.

And yet, that morning, I found that my little text deserved to stay online. I was also happy to discover that *Parisian Gentleman* had received seventeen hits in the first few hours of its short existence. Seventeen hits! Of course, it seems laughable today, but I still think these seventeen strangers who, in the wee small hours of the morning, chanced upon an obscure blog that hadn't been up for more than a couple of hours literally changed my life and made me want to keep going.

Six years on and millions of hits later, *Parisian Gentleman* has become a fully fledged online magazine dedicated to men's style, with an international readership. The title of the tome you hold in your hands is the name that was picked hastily for the blog, now a real book by one of my favourite publishers, Thames & Hudson.

Whatever happened? Well, a small revolution. Following the lead of a few tweed addicts, a bunch of Milanese buttonhole devotees and a small community of shoe aficionados, men seem to have awakened from thirty years of stylistic lethargy and rediscovered the pleasure of beautiful clothes and elegance as a way of life. These 'sartorialists', as they like to call themselves, come from such innovative forums as *London Lounge* or *Style Forum*. They are now an informal but powerful online community with a worldwide influence.

After the success of such television series as *Mad Men* and *Boardwalk Empire*, the 'sartorialists' created a global movement devoted to classic men's style. Many blogs emerged as a result, including *Permanent Style* in London, *A Suitable Wardrobe* and *Gentleman's Gazette* in the United States and *Parisian Gentleman* in Paris – blogs with an international readership on an equal footing with those of the great traditional print magazines.

But while women's glossy fashion magazines continue to extol star designers and models, the sartorial blogosphere has brought to light heroes of a new kind – not designers or artistic directors, but tailors, master shirt- and shoemakers. We're not talking about Karl Largerfeld, Hedi Slimane or Marc Jacobs, but about Lorenzo Cifonelli, Pierre Corthay, Marc de Luca, Anthony Delos and Jean-Claude Colban. Whereas the last three decades were single-mindedly concerned with the pioneering genius and occasionally wild boldness of fashion designers, we

are now rediscovering the subtle workmanship and timeless creations of genuinely creative artisans. These are people who, far from the surreal gloss and tinsel of haute couture, have been making clothes, shoes, perfumes and other essentials for thousands of elegant gentlemen from Paris and elsewhere – and have been doing so, some of them, for three or four generations.

In these glorious times of stylistic renaissance, Paris, the world capital of fashion and haute couture for women, is at last celebrating its own artisans, the low-key family businesses that have been working to make men elegant for more than a century. These historical Paris *maisons* have attracted such distinguished patrons as Claude Debussy, Charles Baudelaire, Sacha Guitry, Jean Cocteau, and also Andy Warhol, Marcello Mastroianni and Philippe Noiret, who remained loyal to them all their lives.

This book does not provide a complete list of all the great *maisons* in Paris that deal in classic men's style. It is rather the outcome of years of fastidious work, a tribute to these large- or small-scale firms, world-famous or unknown, that keep creating luxurious suits, shoes and shirts, trunks and ties, perfumes, spectacles and handkerchiefs that stand out as the most beautiful in the world. It is also a tribute to the men and women in tailors', shoemakers' and trunk-makers' workshops who anonymously produce exquisite articles (sometimes destined to sport an illustrious brand name) that express the extent of their skill and the depth of their very soul.

Hugo Jacomet

INTRODUCTION

This book is here to right a wrong. Paris, the world capital of luxury, fashion and haute couture, bristling with names that shine as beacons of timeless elegance, has long been exalted for its acclaimed heroes and pioneers – Coco Chanel, Yves Saint Laurent, Christian Dior – who contributed much to the style and beauty of women.

But the worldwide reputation and pre-eminence of women as emblems of French or Parisian refinement ('French' and 'Parisian' being virtually synonymous in the minds of most people outside France) have cast a shadow over another aspect of our national treasure: the sheer excellence of the French artisans and boutiques devoted to men's style.

Indeed, the world of fashion shows, star models and illustrious designers stands in stark contrast with the hushed and meditative atmosphere of master tailors' and shoemakers' workshops. They seem worlds apart, devoid of common codes; they do not speak the same language, and certainly do not share the same customers. Yet the French capital is home to many dazzling houses to which contemporary men's style is indebted and whose renown and influence are every bit as commendable as those of the *maisons de haute couture* for women.

Being sandwiched between two heavyweights of men's style – England to the north and Italy to the south – France has benefited from its porous borders and the proximity of its Italian and British counterparts. One doesn't have to be a specialist to realize that many household names of bespoke tailoring have a Roman ring (Cifonelli, Camps de Luca, Smalto), while the most beautiful Parisian workshop of bespoke shoes, John Lobb (a subsidiary of the Hermès group), is one of the most prestigious British names on the planet.

Nevertheless, it is high time to look beyond intellectual and historical caricatures of French style. France has done more than just import the art of fine shoes from Northamptonshire and the art of fine tailoring from the bay of Naples or the inner suburbs of Rome. As we discover in this book, that view is not only a cliché but also

The author wearing a bespoke double-breasted suit by Cifonelli, a bespoke shirt by Courtot and a tie by Marc Guyot.

Opposite, clockwise from top left: An artisan at Maison Bonnet crafts a pair of bespoke spectacles; Thierry Wasser, the 'nose' of the iconic Parisian perfumery house Guerlain; Dimitri Gomez, master bootmaker; and Marc de Luca, master tailor at Camps de Luca.

in many instances a historical mistake. For example, most people believe that London's Jermyn Street shirt-makers founded luxury shirt-making for men, but it was actually a French establishment from Paris, the *maison* Charvet, that invented the modern shirt with the turned-down collar. The first Royal Warrant received in 1869 by Edouard Charvet from the Prince of Wales (later King Edward VII) is marked in French 'Chemisier in Paris', for this highly specialized type of business had not yet been invented in Great Britain and the English 'shirt-maker' simply did not exist.

We will also discover that, during the 1950s, while Vincenzo Attolini (Gennaro Rubinacci's star head cutter in Naples) was working on the famous dropped Neapolitan shoulder that was to transform contemporary jackets radically, Arturo Cifonelli and Joseph Camps were busy working out what would become famous as the cigarette shoulder and the 'French notch' lapel, two important emblems of the Parisian school of bespoke tailoring. In addition, when Hermès acquired John Lobb – the crown jewel of British shoemaking – in 1976, it meant taking control of the outstanding workshop at 24 Faubourg Saint-Honoré in Paris, which had been manned since 1902 by French master bootmakers.

Such charming anecdotes and fascinating historical tales are not gathered from glossy brochures narrating the official legend of famous brands, nor copied from the fawning eulogies written by media that supposedly specializes in luxury. Rather, they were fastidiously hand-picked (as they should be) over the course of several years spent talking to or interviewing some of the most compelling characters of the hushed – or should I say *feutré*? – world of men's clothing in Paris. It meant observing and carefully studying a closed and quiet world. As a result, despite its beautiful pictures, I hope that *The Parisian Gentleman* is more than simply a catalogue of fine objects made by fine artisans performing the fine gestures of their fine craft for the finest houses in Paris.

The book is less than complete as a directory of Paris brands and boutiques. My aim was not to review extensively the many houses that deal in men's style with the breathtaking skill that abounds in Paris. I chose instead to concentrate on a few painstakingly selected *maisons*, choices that were dictated by nothing else than my own taste, but that I hope will represent the epitome of the Parisian style.

It may sound frivolous to talk about welts and gussets, cigarette shoulders and Parisian heels, heavy silk and hidden colours or French notch lapels, patented clasps, tortoiseshell inlays and hem-rolling, but all these stories hold a powerful poetic sway that I have tried to set off throughout the chapters so luminously illustrated by my very dear friend Andy Julia's exceptional pictures.

This book is also a cry for help. For, despite the superb pictures, the fabulous luxury objects and the traditional artisans' skill that abound here, there is no escaping reality. Since the beginning of the century, classic men's style has enjoyed a vibrant phase of unprecedented renewal. All over the world men are passionately rediscovering the pleasure of bespoke tailoring. But in spite of all that, France is suffering – and that is a great understatement – from an extensive vocational crisis regarding manual jobs in general and, more particularly, those in leather and textile crafts. While luxury luggage, bespoke suits and footwear made in Paris are arousing the keenest interest around the world and even garnering new attention from a generation of young men eager to hone their personal elegance, it has become increasingly difficult for the relevant businesses to find skilled workers to respond to the developing demand.

How can this be so in the country of the Compagnons du Devoir? These crafts are demanding and take a long time to learn, but they are noble and rewarding. It is difficult to understand why the French are not interested in learning them, as young Italians or Britons are. Why should it be such a battle for these workshops to find piece-makers or shoe-last makers – even beginners?

As the master bootmaker Pierre Corthay (himself a former Compagnon du Devoir) remarked in my documentary film *La Beauté du geste* (2012), France is snobbish about manual jobs. The parents of secondary-school pupils may claim that they love artisans and buy only their high-end products, but they would not dare encourage their offspring to do anything but go to the best universities to study literature or mathematics.

What will happen if the renewal and development of bespoke suits and shoes continue their course, as is most likely? When the *grandes maisons* can no longer find piece-makers, tailors, seamstresses, cutters, pattern-makers, last-makers and shoemakers to cater to the growing needs of new customers?

It is thus urgent, in France more than anywhere else, to rescue these treasured national trades and to foster apprenticeships, making it easier for young people to train in the fine crafts of shoemaking, tailoring, shirt- and luggage-making and not become mired in the solitary maze of technical education, too often regarded as a dead end for those who fail to stay on the main track of general education.

I still cannot understand why Paris does not boast a national academy of tailoring, an institute for traditional shoemaking or a college devoted to the French art of trunk-making. It would help these fine crafts to be acknowledged as a legitimate artistic and technical education, and attract young talent in France so as to ensure the transmission of the unique skills that are so vital to the country's image and influence throughout the world.

Internet and e-learning will not help with the most demanding techniques, which can be acquired only by observing and repeating the gestures time and time again with a mentor. As the African proverb says, 'When an old man dies, a library burns.' With its worldwide reputation for luxury articles, passing on the skills of perfumers, tailors, goldsmiths, lacquer artists and shirt-, shoe- and trunk-makers should be a national cause for France. Should this book help, however modestly, to attract the attention of young people and make them realize the beauty of those professions, which have such a bright future, I shall be a happy writer.

While we hope for that blessed future, though, the sartorialist revolution is in full swing. Parisian gentlemen of all generations have never been so stylish.

1

PARISIAN BESPOKE TAILORING

Page 22

The Camps de Luca
bespoke salon,
looking into the
bespoke workshop.

Opposite

Detail of a bespoke
Key West sports jacket
by Cifonelli.

Bespoke tailoring has enjoyed a global revival of interest over the past few years, and gentlemen in every country are rediscovering the ultra-sophisticated and fascinating field of bespoke suits.

Undeniably, the renewal in this field has seen England and Italy take the lion's share of this rapidly expanding territory, thanks to such major poles of attraction as London, Milan, Rome and Naples. Until very recently, Paris could no longer claim to be a major city of men's tailoring. Unlike England and Italy, France had trouble handling the evolution of the clothing industry and the competition of mass production in the 1960s, so that local tailors gradually disappeared, leaving only a few luxury boutiques in Paris with a rich and faithful clientele.

It is no wonder that with only a handful of bespoke specialists left at the turn of the century, Paris was not able to put up much of a fight against the exceptional – not to say anachronistic – concentration of tailors in Savile Row, the sanctum of British tailoring, or the Naples *sartoria* in the riotous backstreets of the former capital of the Kingdom of Naples and the Two Sicilies. And yet, just a look at the history of tailoring from the 1950s onwards shows that Paris boasted names that resonate today as stars of the profession: Arturo Cifonelli, Joseph Camps, Mario de Luca and later Francesco Smalto and the Grimbert brothers.

In order to understand the world of tailoring, give due credit to the Parisian masters of that era and fully enjoy this book, one should take into account a few basic facts. In the field of tailoring, France is rather wedged between two star countries, England and Italy, each with its own take on men's suits.

On the one hand, British tailors – gathered on Savile Row, a small street in London less than a mile long – represent a classic and sober approach to tailoring with typical British understatement. One might view it as a subtle way to imply more than meets the eye. This visual understatement is so central to British tailoring that, according to an old joke, if someone pays you a compliment about your suit your tailor has been too obvious and has failed in his attempt at quiet elegance. After ten years spent roving around tailors' showrooms everywhere on the planet (including Savile Row), however, I can assure you that this witty fable doesn't hold, for, *bien sûr*, I have never seen a gentleman offended by a pleasant word from a connoisseur about his latest bespoke suit, and even less by one from a beautiful lady.

What the story does show, however, is that in London traditions are no laughing matter. Except for a few *enfants terribles*, such as Tommy Nutter and his

Arturo Cifonelli in the 1950s: one
of the greatest tailors of all time.

The legendary master
tailor Joseph Camps
teaches students,
including the young
Francesco Smalto (to
his left) and Emanuel
Ungaro (to his right,
in the white shirt).

Joseph Camps packs
for a foreign trip for
customer fittings in the
late 1960s.

partner in crime, Edward Sexton – who tried to rock
things up during the 1970s, attempting to shake the
Golden Mile out of its torpor with a little help from
the Beatles, who had set up their Apple studio at
3 Savile Row – nothing has really changed since these
establishments were founded in the late nineteenth
century. English tailoring stemmed from military
tailoring, and houses such as Gieves & Hawkes and
Dege & Skinner still contribute to that field. They
offer more or less structured shapes, but the general
spirit leans towards sober austerity. The shoulders
tend to be slightly padded and the waist fitted.
Fabrics are usually rather thick (the local weather
is a factor, rendering such tailors heaven for lovers
of tweed and flannel) and jackets are on the rigid
side. There is a gravity to this concept of elegance,
something punctilious and flawless that is in keeping
with the local tradition. The emblematic names are
Henry Poole, Huntsman and Anderson & Sheppard,
an advocate of 'soft tailoring'. This interpretation of
bespoke tailoring, which leaves more room for the

chest, was invented by Frederick Scholte, a Dutch
cutter working on Savile Row at the beginning of
the twentieth century, when he created a suit for the
Prince of Wales, the future Duke of Windsor.

Italian tailors, on the other hand, have never
been clustered in a single location. They were
scattered across Italy, and, after the war, following
twenty years of fascism and isolation, they swept
across Europe and the United States. Whether they
come from the Bay of Naples or the suburbs of
Rome, their tailoring style is much more flamboyant
and less rigid than Britain's. In Italy, especially
in Naples, delicate refinement is the rule. Italian
houses deploy all their talent to create suits that
express lightness and grace. 'Understatement'
is certainly not the word to describe the spirit of
Italian tailoring, but Italy can claim its own take
on elegance, which is conveyed by another notion,
sprezzatura. It is a typically Italian way of suggesting
that your attire, however sophisticated and complex,
is actually a chance happening and not the result

of hard work – a kind of modest and ironically elaborate Latin nonchalance.

In Italy, fashion is the man's realm, even when it comes to classic men's suits. Despite the bleak economic streak that has plagued the country for many years, Italian *sartoria* still reign supreme over the clothing industry, whether luxury or mass-produced ready-made clothing. Bespoke tailoring is still ubiquitous, especially in Naples, a city that has managed to promote its expertise with romantic efficiency.

The famous Neapolitan shoulder, whose construction without padding (*su camisia*) reminds one of a shirt, was invented in 1959 by the star head cutter Vincenzo Attolini when he was working for the no less famous Rubinacci *sartoria*. It caused a revolution in men's suiting as it presented a radically new alternative to British style – a relaxed figure and a natural elegance impishly breaking the codes so staunchly defended by the British. The shoulder can be structured (as is done in Milan or Rome) or dropped (as in Naples), but all Italian suits from proper tailors share this graceful elegance. The renowned names in men's tailoring come from Naples (Mariano Rubinacci, Gennaro Solito, Antonio Panico), Florence (Antonio Liverano) and Milan (A. Caraceni).

The Paris School's Founding Fathers: Arturo Cifonelli and Joseph Camps

Great Parisian men's tailors were long overshadowed by English and Italian workshops. They did not enjoy an equivalent renown until the mid-2000s, since when a growing number of elegant gentlemen have rediscovered the city's bespoke tailors. The greatest among them have even aroused a keen interest that has reached the international sartorial community.

The two major modern figures of Parisian tailoring are Arturo Cifonelli, who comes from Italy, and Joseph Camps, of Spanish origin. The former, who set up his establishment in rue Marbeuf in 1926, had a more subdued and less turbulent career than his Spanish counterpart, but his technical contribution to the art of tailoring has proved as essential and received as much admiration, both in France and internationally.

Arturo Cifonelli learned his craft from his father, Giuseppe, in the family workshop in Rome,

then went to the Minister's Cutting Academy in London. He invented a distinct silhouette and shoulder structure that became famous worldwide. Taking the opposite direction from the Neapolitan tradition of 'soft tailoring', he polished a style based on precision and astounding dexterity, enabling his jackets to have a perfect fit as well as perfect freedom of movement. The Cifonelli style has been kept alive by the invaluable work of subsequent generations of the family – Adriano, Lorenzo and Massimo – and has gained international popularity. Its signature shoulder, acclaimed for its light structure and slightly pitched sleevehead, is now famous as the 'Cifonelli shoulder'.

Joseph Camps is from Spain – or rather, from Catalonia. In 1956 he was one of the founders of the Groupe des Cinq, a unique initiative to enhance the profile of men's haute couture and stand up for traditional tailoring against the invasion of mass-produced ready-to-wear clothing. In the 1960s he stood out as the foremost practitioner of Parisian bespoke tailoring. The Groupe (Camps, André Bardot, Max Evzeline, Charles Austen and Mario de Luca) presented haute couture collections every year until 1970 with a specific Parisian cut and style in mind. They finally split up when they became too old to put up with the constant bickering – master tailors have always been known for their strong characters.

Joseph Camps and Mario de Luca

It was in such an eventful context that the talented but unassuming Mario de Luca, a young tailor who had trained in Rome and Milan and had moved to Paris in 1948, met the Spanish master. The encounter would prove to be a turning point for both men, whose legendary partnership was to be immediately successful with the foundation of Camps de Luca in 1969.

The creative and ebullient Camps, obsessed with his research on measurement, was a great virtuoso and a passionate pioneer, but with a keener interest in technical innovation than in running a business. Conversely, Mario de Luca was not only an ardent lover of Italian style but also had a fine business head and skill at management. Together they created Camps de Luca, which is still an institution of Parisian bespoke tailoring under the leadership of Marc de Luca (Mario's son) and his own two sons.

Camps de Luca suits typically display a well-structured figure, but not excessively so, with a slight roll on the sleevehead and a fitted waist. Their other characteristic is the famous 90-degree lapel notch, the 'Camps notch' that went on to be developed by Francesco Smalto in his own *maison*.

Joseph Camps was not just, with Arturo Cifonelli, one of the greatest tailors of his generation. He was also a mentor to many tailors who made their own names after training with him. His most talented disciple was Smalto, but Henri Urban and Emanuel Ungaro also learned from him, as did Claude Rousseau and Gabriel Gonzalez, who were employed by Cifonelli years later.

Francesco Smalto and the Grimbert Brothers

Francesco Smalto started out in Joseph Camps's workshop as fourth cutter in 1957, becoming head cutter in 1961. He was the most prominent among the second generation of the Camps disciples, a real school in its own right. He had arrived in Paris from Calabria in 1951 with a firm goal in mind: to become 'the greatest men's tailor of his times'. He was indeed destined to be part of the pantheon of national treasures in men's style, and created a very virile figure, a strong structure featuring a rolled 'egg-head' shoulder and a geometric notched lapel, often called *cran parisien*, a direct borrowing from the Camps notch. He quickly became the favourite tailor of many stars and heads of state, including the king of Morocco, one of his most faithful customers.

Smalto had a very modern approach to line and texture, and, following Pierre Cardin, he even dabbled in futuristic design in the early 1970s. Keen to transmit his skill in the same spirit as his Catalan master, he invented a new way of taking measurements and designing a first draft for jackets (with soft plastic templates) that enables the company that bears his name to carry on making bespoke suits in keeping with the methods of its admired founder.

On the opposite bank of the Seine, meanwhile, far from the boisterous Groupe des Cinq and the wild tailors of the Right Bank, is a quiet establishment that has become a major boutique for elegant Parisians: Arnys. It was created in 1926 by Jankel Grimbert, who set up shop in 1933 in the rue de Sèvres. The firm, whose clientele is almost exclusively Parisian, was among the very first *maisons* to offer luxury ready-to-wear clothing in the 1950s, alongside traditional bespoke tailoring.

This unique family business is often regarded by the cognoscenti as the only firm to have a distinctly Parisian style devoid of Italian or Spanish influence. This style has been the unofficial signature of the Paris political intelligentsia for more than thirty years. The firm's low-key elegance, restrained rather than showy, is embodied by its casual-chic collections of easy-to-wear clothes. Its iconic piece, the Forestière jacket, was created in 1947 for the architect Le Corbusier. This beautiful jacket with a mandarin collar was inspired by the world of hunting and gamekeeping. It has stood the test of time and is still lovingly featured in the catalogue of Berluti, the owner of Arnys since 2012.

In Search of the Parisian Style

Claiming the existence of a specifically Parisian style whose influence and magnitude equalled the British and Italian styles would clearly be excessive, and in a book such as this could be taken as the sign of a Gallic-centred point of view. As a matter of fact, except for the remarkable case of Arnys, it is impossible to deny the overwhelming Italian influence that still reigns supreme among Parisian tailors, whose names would not appear out of place in the telephone directories of Milan, Rome or Naples. And yet these firms have gradually broken free from that rich legacy to offer their own dazzling take on the famous Parisian 'chic', in the process garnering praise from their peers on Savile Row and the Via Chiaia.

CIFONELLI

Parisian Tailoring Icon

Cifonelli has been the icon and point of reference for Parisian bespoke tailoring for decades. It has become a world-famous institution, one that stands as a beacon for men's sartorial style.

Whereas other firms lost their souls (or rather sold their souls) under the combined assaults of mass culture and the financial appeal of corporate Eldorado, the house on the rue Marbeuf has managed to reinvent itself relentlessly without ever showing off, sustaining its legendary record of excellence and punctiliousness in every detail of every suit it produces. Tucked away in its hushed and cosy *salon*, replete with studious zeal, the boutique boasts forty people who work exclusively by hand and turn out about 900 suits every year, each one realized to the exacting standards of traditional tailoring craft.

The Founding Fathers (and Sons): Giuseppe, Arturo and Adriano

Founded in 1880 in Rome by Giuseppe Cifonelli, the family business really took off thanks to Giuseppe's son Arturo, who remains one of the great geniuses of tailoring in the eyes of connoisseurs.

In the early twentieth century the Mecca of tailoring was London, and would-be tailors flocked there to learn English techniques of cutting and sewing. It was only logical that young Arturo Cifonelli should learn his trade at the respectable Minister's Cutter Academy in London. He returned to Italy with his degree in 1911, to take over the family business. This early training has meant that measurements at Cifonelli's are always taken in inches, unlike most other French and Italian tailors, which work in metric units.

In 1926, as Fascist boots were making themselves heard on the pavements of Rome and elsewhere in Italy, Arturo Cifonelli realized that his high-society clientele would soon flee, and so decided to set up shop in Paris. The eponymous boutique opened in 1936 at 31 rue Marbeuf, establishing itself as one of the first houses of men's clothing in the 'Golden Triangle' of luxury shops and haute couture, a stone's throw from the Champs-Elysées.

Arturo remained famous for his undisputed talent but also for his notoriously exacting demands. His daughter Liliane, who at the time of writing is still in charge of the company (with her brother Adriano), recalls telling episodes:

Cifonelli's Canadian sports jacket is a sophisticated garment with chest pleats, inspired by traditional Canadian hunting jackets.

When someone showed [him] the work they'd done on a jacket, they would always be very anxious, for they knew that my father was extremely demanding. I've often seen him slashing at a piece of work that the man had been working on for fifty hours, just because he didn't like it or because he thought it was not in line with the house style. Working with him wasn't easy, but those who stuck with him never regretted it – he was a master. Someone difficult to get along with but a true genius.

When Arturo died, in 1972, his son Adriano took over. I am lucky enough to know Adriano personally, and in my honest opinion he is one of the great underrated names of Parisian style, with Denis Colban of Charvet. Adriano lost the use of his legs in a car accident in 1977, but that did not deter him from perpetuating the very recognizable style established by his father. (In the early 1980s he was even celebrated on French national television as the first paraplegic to ski a very difficult run in the French Alps, using a special device.) Today Adriano still works faithfully at his bench in the cutting workshop, keeping a watchful

eye on his nephew Massimo and his son Lorenzo, cutting hundreds of the finest suits in the world every year.

Adriano Cifonelli is part of a generation of old-school taciturn Italian tailors who rarely compliment the younger generation. I have come across that tight-lipped attitude in Italy among tailors and fabric experts. The talented and famous Francesco Barberis Canonico, artistic director of the eponymous fabric house, told me that it is not uncommon for Italian fathers to be (more than) a little harsh on their sons, leaving them to improve on their own, giving only the minimum of instruction and rarely giving a word of praise for their work.

Although Adriano is immensely proud of Lorenzo, who is now regarded as one of the greatest tailors and designers in the world, he will never compliment him in the presence of a customer, preferring to point out the details that could be improved on. It's a matter of education and tradition.

The New Generation: Lorenzo and Massimo

In the early 1990s Lorenzo and Massimo, the grandsons of Arturo Cifonelli, took over

Adriano Cifonelli (Arturo's son and Lorenzo's father), one of the unsung heroes of Parisian tailoring, is still at his cutting table, helping his son and nephew to cut and design some of the most exquisite men's garments in the world.

Massimo (top left) and Lorenzo Cifonelli (centre right) are pictured at work in the legendary Cifonelli workshop close to the Champs-Elysées. In this traditional bespoke house, every pattern for every garment is unique and still designed, cut and sewn by hand. It represents bespoke tailoring at its summit.

Cifonelli's signature double-breasted blazer. On this '6 on 1' jacket, the last row of buttons (including the active one) is positioned slightly higher than is normal in a jacket of this kind.

Clockwise from top left: Chest and arm pockets of the Canadian jacket; the chest patch pocket with gussets and flap of the Qilian jacket, made from yak wool; the refined gusseted and half-belted back of the Stirling jacket; suede inserts in the pockets and slanted sleeve buttonholes on the Vintage jacket.

'Cifonelli, Young Man, Go to Cifonelli'
by Wei Koh

The best-dressed man I've ever met wore a Cifonelli suit. I was in the lift at the Hôtel Plaza Athénée in Paris when in walked a silver-haired gentleman in the most miraculous dove-grey flannel double-breasted suit I have ever seen. It shimmered – no, positively radiated – with perfection. I noticed that sewn subtly beside his buttonhole was the red thread that symbolized his membership of France's Légion d'Honneur. But even then, I couldn't help but ask who his tailor was. He looked at me and said one word: 'Cifonelli'.

This is the story I think back on as, several years later, I watch my own jacket take shape under the watchful eye of Massimo Cifonelli. Massimo is softly spoken, studious and focused – in the way he moves, the way he acts and the way he speaks. When you know him, you realize that this is an extension of the rigid pursuit of precision and perfection that has occupied his life. He and his cousin Lorenzo, who is a brilliant tailor and also one of the best designers working in classic men's elegance today, run the three-generations-old Cifonelli atelier on rue Marbeuf.

Massimo's parents live across the street, and his father is still one of the first people in the shop every day. I've come to realize that Massimo is one of tailoring's greatest technical geniuses. As I observe him deconstructing the backneck and collar of my jacket, he explains to me the fundamental technical findings of his grandfather Arturo Cifonelli, the firm's founder, when it came to reconciling comfort and shape – or, to be more pedantic, function and form – in the tailored jacket: 'Our grandfather did a tremendous amount of research on this. How do you keep a jacket slim and close-fitting, but still allow for total freedom of movement? What he arrived at were several principles. The first is that he liked the chest of his jackets to be very clean.' Indeed, the Cifonelli chest is probably the leanest in bespoke tailoring – so much so that, at first, you wonder how you will fit your mobile phone and wallet into the chest pockets and still be able to move. But fear not – you will.

'The second is that the back of the coat is wider by several centimetres than the front,' Massimo continues. 'This added material has to be eased

the business. They developed it in a major way, especially when they started a sixteen-year collaboration with Hermès (1992–2008), and by the mid-2000s Cifonelli was established as one of the greatest houses in the world.

I think a gentleman should have one main tailor in his life, and Cifonelli is mine. It is difficult to speak objectively about the tailor in your life, though, and so I am deferring to my good friend Wei Koh – founder of the revered magazine *The Rake* – who has written the following remarks.

manually into the hand-sewn shoulder seam and then ironed so that it is flush with the coat front. 'The third is that our armhole is very high and sits close to the body.' Not only is the Cifonelli armhole the highest in the business, but also, to be more specific, the front part of the armhole is cut very close to the chest to isolate completely the deltoid in the sleevehead. As a result, the sleevehead of the Cifonelli jacket actually appears to be pitched or angled slightly in towards the chest. That demonstrates this house's unique ability to sculpt in three dimensions, when most tailors operate in two.

'Fourth, we create a soft, natural shoulder with very little padding, and shape the sleevehead using a form we call "La Cigarette".' It was the combination of the slightly pitched sleeve with La Cigarette that motivated fashion Svengali Karl Lagerfeld to announce: 'I could recognize a Cifonelli shoulder from a distance of a hundred metres.'

But it is totally incorrect to equate La Cigarette with the British roped sleevehead. The former uses layers of hand-wadding, combined with stretching and shaping to create a sensual yet heroic dome-shaped cupola without any underlying structure. In contrast, the roped sleevehead actually uses a length of rope that is placed over the shoulder from front to back to create a ridged shape. However, this rope ends up occupying space that should ideally be kept empty for the shoulder to move freely. It also tends to add undesirable rigidity.

As such, the roped sleevehead is an aesthetic conceit, while the Cifonelli Cigarette is, as with all the house's innovations, both functional and beautiful. Why? Because this unique shape allows the added material at the sleevehead to become part

Cifonelli's world-acclaimed bespoke sports jackets. (From left to right:) The '6 on 1' double-breasted blazer, the Canadian, the Vintage, the Qilian and the Stirling.

of the jacket's structural form, rather than hanging limply or in pleats, as is seen in British drape or Neapolitan tailoring respectively. It creates volume in the sleevehead for better freedom of movement, but brilliantly hides that volume in what appears to be an aesthetic decision.

The final, and perhaps most important, principle of a Cifonelli jacket is hidden. As he describes it, Massimo allows himself a smile: 'What people often don't realize is that all these elements – the chest, the front of the coat, the back, the shoulder – are anchored by the collar and backneck of the jacket.'

The idea of commissioning your first Cifonelli jacket is, in some ways, an intimidating one. Most tailors will show you a few examples of their house style, or perhaps you've already admired it on an acquaintance and your choice relates primarily to

style and fabric. Walk into Cifonelli, however, and Lorenzo will show you an endless array of some of the most exquisite clothes on Earth, each created with the house's signature magical union between shape and comfort, but in seemingly endless variations. Lorenzo is dynamic, buzzing with almost electric energy and boundless intelligence.

Adriano cut clothes for François Mitterrand and Marcello Mastroianni. 'The basic structure of our clothes is a starting point,' says Lorenzo, 'but at Cifonelli, we encourage you to dream, to think about who you want to be, and we will find a way to express this in what we make for you.'

Among Lorenzo's most dazzling offerings are the Canadienne, a sports jacket with chest pleats inspired by traditional Canadian hunting jackets; the Vintage, a dress coat with a suede-trimmed, rowing-boat-shaped breast pocket and suede-backed patch pockets;

the Travel Jacket, which is crafted from Tibetan yak wool; and the Stirling, a demi-point-lapel sports jacket with leather-trimmed flap pockets. You can revel for hours in the extraordinary creations on display, your mind reeling at the endless possibilities. But what is impressive with Cifonelli is that every garment you receive from them is nothing less than perfect.

I had come for one specific reason, and that was to have Lorenzo's iconic double-breasted blazer made for me. This is a six-button jacket that fastens at the bottom, and follows a style that I've always wanted to adopt, having seen it on many of the world's most stylish men – including the Duke of Kent, Fred Astaire, Ralph Lauren and Luca Cordero di Montezemolo – but I have never been able to wear it comfortably.

While I love the lengthening effect to the lapel, I can't get over the way your tie and shirtfront almost spill out with the low buttoning point when you sit. But on Lorenzo's jacket, the last row of buttons is brought higher, similar to that of a four-button dinner jacket, so the result is far less sloppy. What it loses in dégagé elan, it gains in structural sleekness. Flourishing from the bottom row of buttons are the most beautifully shaped double-breasted lapels on the planet, evincing just the perfect amount of long, curved belly before flaring out into ultra-wide, archetypically heroic, high-gorge points. For the first time, I didn't have to struggle to explain my preference for a high breast pocket, because Cifonelli already places it at exactly the right point.

Look closely and you'll see that the opening of the Cifonelli double-breasted jacket seems elegantly to embrace the curvature of the male chest, rather than falling across it in the style of a kimono or bathrobe, as lesser double-breasted jackets do. Flip up the Cifonelli lapel and you'll see why. The lapel is not part of the jacket front, but formed from a second piece of fabric that is joined perfectly along a seam that follows the curvature of the male chest. 'If you want to create a double-breasted jacket with an opening that perfectly follows the contours of the chest, you have to do this,' says Lorenzo. 'But very few tailors would be willing, or have the ability.'

Amazingly, a few days after the initial fitting, Lorenzo had already created a fitting canvas from scratch for me. 'Some tailors will use a premade block on you to help them visualize,' he explains,

'but for me, I must always start from scratch and build the canvas with the person I've fitted [while it's] fresh in my mind.' Despite having one of the biggest teams of in-house tailors in the world, Lorenzo supervises every stage of the unique Cifonelli process, which includes hand-worked chests, handmade seams and finishing throughout, and exquisite Milanese buttonholes.

The Lorenzo Cifonelli double-breasted jacket is shorter than most, high-waisted and fitted before flaring into a beautiful skirt. The two blazers that result from my visit – one in bird's-eye blue wool and the other in a blue silk-linen blend – are among the most consistently complimented clothes I have ever worn.

Each time I receive a positive remark, I'm reminded of that evening, in the lift of the Plaza Athénée, when I ran into that particularly elegant elderly gentleman. After he divulged the name of his tailor, I paused for a while before saying: 'Sir, I hope I haven't offended you, as there is a school of thought that says you should notice only the man and never the clothes.'

He chuckled: 'That is a school of thought perpetuated by people with mediocre clothing. Cifonelli, young man – go to Cifonelli.'

W. K.

Ready-to-wear and World Development

In 2014, as Cifonelli enjoyed worldwide interest for its exceptional bespoke production, it launched a high-quality ready-to-wear line of clothes with a new partner. For this new phase of its development, the firm called on John Vizzone, the former artistic director at Ralph Lauren, and started working with a small manufacturing unit in Naples in Italy to translate the bespoke house style into ready-to-wear, enabling more gentlemen around the world to have the Cifonelli experience. This is a new chapter for a company that has managed to keep a signature style alive and make it grow with graceful passion to become a truly world-class leader in men's style.

Cifonelli, young men – go to Cifonelli!

CAMPS DE LUCA

Quintessentially Parisian

The famous Parisian menswear house Camps de Luca was born in 1969 when two renowned tailors, the Catalan Joseph Camps and the Italian Mario de Luca, joined forces. Camps was among the most admired and respected master tailors of his time, but in spite of that, his contribution to modern tailoring has remained strangely underrated, for reasons I shall explain. Mario's son Marc de Luca, who is in charge of the company today, still calls Joseph 'Maître Camps', as he remains an eminent part of the legend of French tailoring (alongside Arturo Cifonelli). He trained the crème de la crème of French bespoke cutters, figures such as Francesco Smalto, Henri Urban, Claude Rousseau and Gabriel Gonzalez (who still works at Cifonelli's).

The question to ask is why Joseph Camps never enjoyed the same kind of fame outside France as did Smalto, for example, who was among his apprentices in the early 1950s before becoming one of his star cutters. It is also strange that no book or exhibition has ever told the story of this Catalan tailor, who was a major contributor to French and international tailoring.

There are, in my opinion, two reasons for Camps's lack of fame. First, he was known to be a genius tailor, but was more interested in his research

and technical innovations than in the management of his own business or in communication. Second, he reached the climax of his career at the worst possible time for a tailor (the late 1960s and the 1970s), and he did not have the time to reach his Holy Grail, what he called 'techno-measure', the precursor of what we would today call industrial measure or made-to-measure.

Mario de Luca was an Italian through and through. He had learned the job with his uncle, a tailor in Atina, in the central Italian region of Lazio, before he moved on to learn the trade with more famous tailors in Rome and Milan. When he came to Paris, in 1948, his sense of fit and his flair for design and style soon made him one of the most sought-after tailors in the city.

In the 1960s de Luca became a member of the Groupe des Cinq, and it was through that association – which presented several collections a year, in the manner of haute couture houses for women – that he met 'Maître Camps' in 1969. The two men decided to work together, and created Camps de Luca. With Camps a technical genius and de Luca a talented tailor who was also good at managing their business, the alliance paid off. Indeed, it gave birth to one of the most prosperous

Advertisement for the Groupe des Cinq, a unique initiative by several famous Parisian tailors to promote their art and to fight the rise of mass production in the 1960s.

Marc de Luca with his two sons (Charles, left, and Julien) – the second and third generation of a family saga begun in 1948 by Mario de Luca. The firm is a Parisian institution of discretion and good taste.

tailoring businesses of the time, boasting more than forty workers and turning out more than a thousand suits a year during the 1970s.

Techno-measure: Joseph Camps's Unfinished Masterwork

In the 1960s, while Camps's business was thriving (it was then still independent from Mario de Luca's), he rushed headlong into a rather whimsical enterprise that was to make his reputation but also put him more than once into a predicament.

Leaving his star cutters, including Francesco Smalto, to deal with his firm's select clientele and produce exceptional handmade suits, Camps had one obsession: to streamline the complex and time-consuming process of taking measurements and creating patterns for suits, and to mechanize traditional bespoke, so to speak, to find a quicker and simpler way of producing suits. The tailor transformed into an engineer, the plumb line replaced the shears and Camps spent most of his time trying to develop his concept. At that moment, most of his cutters left him – the talented Smalto leading the wave – to start their own businesses. They left a critical hole, and inevitably took away some of Camps's customers.

Meeting Mario de Luca and forming a partnership with him was to be the Spanish maestro's salvation. The business, now named Camps de Luca, grew and garnered a great

The legendary master tailor Joseph Camps shares a glass of champagne with his staff in 1955.

Mario de Luca, who created Camps de Luca with Joseph Camps in 1969.

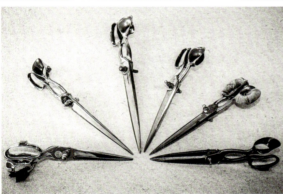

Camps de Luca's atelier is
a place of tradition, with a
collection of original shears
from various periods.

reputation, especially in certain spheres, such as
show business (their most fêted customer was the
singer Claude François, an idol of the 1960s and
1970s in France).

But Camps was still focused on his idea and
intent on keeping his own workshop on the Champs-
Elysées so as to carry on his research and create
the new mode of production, the first of its kind in
tailoring – 'techno-measure'. His plan was to carry
out a trial fitting on his customers using a basic
jacket, and then to use that standard cut as a basis
for each new jacket, mechanizing some of the
steps of the process.

It was an excellent concept: it opened the door
of the tailor to people who were either in a rush or
devoid of the means needed for a real tailor's job – or
both. The problem was that this visionary technique
was not yet up to scratch. It was not uncommon
for customers to bring the suits they had had made
with this new technique at Camps's boutique in the
Champs-Elysées to the bespoke Camps de Luca
workshop on place de la Madeleine to have them
altered. It was a huge commercial and financial failure,
as well as a waste of time, and de Luca had no choice,
wise manager that he was, but to put an end to the
experiment and bring the business back to basics.

Some might suggest that Camps's idea was
ahead of its time, but I don't think it was a question
of timing. Rather, such a revolutionary concept
needed a more industrial approach. The tools and

processes that are being used today in industrial measure or made-to-measure, of which 'techno-measure' was indeed the precursor, were required to carry it through. So we should give Camps his due and acknowledge his visionary approach.

Quintessentially Parisian

For many connoisseurs of bespoke tailoring, Camps de Luca is one of the two or three houses that are the ultimate embodiment of the classic Parisian style. It might seem strange to talk about Parisian style when discussing a tailoring house born out of the association of a Spaniard and an Italian, yet Camps de Luca has gradually established itself as a specifically Parisian tailor whose approach is in line with French staples: a concave roped shoulder (*very* Parisian, that), a high sleevehead, a somewhat protruding chest with a slight drape, a defined waist and high pockets. The general appearance of a Camps de Luca suit – more structured than an Italian suit and with a closer fit than a British one – is so charismatic that it inevitably attracts the eye.

There is also the famous Camps de Luca lapel notch, sometimes called *cran parisien* or *cran tailleur* ('French notch' or 'tailor's notch'), 'frogmouth' or 'fishmouth', or *bocca di lupo* ('wolfmouth'). The Camps notch has been under the spotlight for the past few years, and many have attempted to copy it.

It was designed by Camps and de Luca, and remains a strong house feature. A Camps de Luca jacket with a *cran tailleur* radiates unique character. The notch is cut with two 90-degree angles, but is not quite symmetrical, since the upper line (near the collar, called *contre-anglaise*) is slightly shorter than the lower (the *anglaise*). This notch is a paragon of balance and a reference point for Parisian and international tailoring.

Claude François and his Famous Suits

During the late 1960s and the 1970s, Claude François was the most popular and idolized artist in France, and the one who received the most media exposure. Renowned for his immaculate looks and exceptional talent as a dancer, he displayed impressive energy and impeccable suits – even when dancing.

Marc de Luca remembers this famous customer quite clearly:

> The secret of the suits we designed for him lay in the very high sleevehead. It enabled the suit to keep its close fit even when he danced and pranced. When he came to see us at our place de la Madeleine boutique, there was always a riot in the whole neighbourhood, up to the stairs where young girls would fight to get close to him. My father Mario and Claude François had a truly deep relationship as friends.

At Camps de Luca's bespoke atelier in Paris, every garment is cut and sewn by hand according to the gospel of bespoke tailoring.

Overleaf

Marc de Luca, one of the greatest master tailors in the world, photographed in 2014 by Andy Julia in Camps de Luca's former bespoke salon overlooking the place de la Madeleine.

As only a real traditional
bespoke house will do,
Camps de Luca gives
its customers access to
the most exclusive and
luxurious fabrics in the
world, mainly from the
greatly respected mills of
Italy and Great Britain.

My father knew the whimsical and demanding
personality of Claude François, so he had adopted
the habit of preparing five or six suits in advance
even if [François] hadn't ordered anything, just to
make sure that he would not be taken aback by a
surprise order at the last minute. I remember once
when Claude François asked my father to deliver
five suits he needed to take with him on tour with
only a week's notice – fortunately, they were
already ready to go!

Mario, Marc, Julien and Charles de Luca

Marc de Luca, Mario's son, started out as an
apprentice in 1970 in the firm's workshop on place
de la Madeleine. He was only sixteen, and would
patiently learn for twelve long years all the details
of the complex art of tailoring under the fatherly but
demanding scrutiny of Mario and the other tailors:
stitching, pattern-making, taking measurements and
taking charge of fittings. Every Sunday morning

he would learn the craft of cutting with Maître
Camps, probably one of the best cutters of all
time (with Arturo Cifonelli in Paris, Vincenzo
Attolini in Naples, Domenico Caraceni in Rome
and Colin Hammick in London).

Only in 1982 did Marc officially become a
master tailor himself, when his father entrusted
to him his first client. Traditions and education
are no trifling matter in the de Luca family:
'Father did not want my sons Charles and Julien
to become tailors,' he reminisces, 'as he thought
it was a difficult trade with worrying prospects
at a time when tailors were closing shop one after
the other because of the assaults of ready-to-wear
and industrialization'.

In spite of that, both Marc's sons ended up
in the family business. Charles started out in the
world of luxury restaurants, while Julien chose
finance in London. But eventually they came back
to give their father a hand, and become master
tailors themselves. Cutting corners was of course

Marc de Luca works on a pattern at his cutting table.

The late acclaimed Alain Stark (of Stark & Sons) displays an Immortal uniform, named after the members of the illustrious Académie Française. Each of these coats requires several hundred hours of embroidery work.

out of the question: Mario's grandsons will have to go through a long training period and learn all the tricks of the trade before they can become fully fledged masters.

Marc and his two sons are now in charge of the legacy of this house, whose clientele has dramatically increased once more thanks to the renewed interest of a new generation of gentlemen in bespoke tailoring. The firm's history shows how the beautiful and exacting process of passing things on can be successfully managed through generations devoted to the craft of bespoke tailoring.

Today and Tomorrow

In late 2014 Camps de Luca was forced to leave its historical premises in the place de la Madeleine after forty-five years, because of a luxury hotel project on the same block. At the same time, the tailor Alain Stark, of Stark & Sons in the prestigious rue de la Paix (opposite Cartier, a stone's throw from the place Vendôme), suddenly died at the age of sixty-four,

just as the two companies had been talking about the possibility of getting together. The passing of Stark, who will be sorely missed (not least by me), sped things up. Camps de Luca took over Stark & Sons: its beautiful boutique in rue de la Paix, the workshop and all the employees, tailors and piece-makers.

Stark & Sons enjoys a great reputation in France for making bespoke and ready-to-wear suits as well as parade uniforms and official costumes. For decades it has designed and made the uniform for the illustrious members of the Académie Française, the 'Immortals', the exquisite jacket of which is so richly embroidered with golden leaf motifs that each needs hundreds of hours of work by hand.

Taking over such a highly respected company represents the beginning of a new era for Marc de Luca and his sons. By keeping the Stark & Sons business going, they have chosen to take their first steps in the world of ready-to-wear, as a complement to their traditional bespoke business, which remains the core of the company.

FRANCESCO SMALTO

The Man Who Would be King of Tailors

'Imagine yourself sitting next to a stranger at a dinner. If you notice that his jacket collar does not completely cover his shirt collar, that his sleeves hide his watch without dangling into his soup, you can have an inkling of a Smalto outfit. If you notice that when he stands his jacket is not pointing limply towards the ground, that his trousers fall on to his shoes without hindering his walk, the inkling becomes likeliness. If you dance with him and the fabric is breathtakingly soft and warm, you know you were right. And if you yield to either the stranger or the Smalto outfit, you will notice at dawn that the turn-ups of his trousers are ten times neater, sturdier and nicer than yours.' Françoise Sagan

Francesco Smalto, who died in April 2015 in Marrakech, the city of his heart, stands out as the leading figure among the second generation of the prestigious line of Camps disciples. His flawless career, spanning five decades, established him not only as one of the major tailors of his time but also as one of the first *fashion* tailors for men in history.

In the spirit of his mentor, Joseph Camps, and of Arturo Cifonelli, Smalto was among the first to aim at something beyond the classic bespoke suit in line with tradition. He engaged in a more general aspect of tailoring that had hitherto been the sole preserve of women's tailoring: the silhouette. A true expert of line and proportion who has been unanimously recognized by his peers, Smalto was a unique artist. He went further than his glorious forebears and succeeded where the Groupe des Cinq had failed.

Every year from 1962 he presented two haute couture collections for men, managing to give a new aura to an austere and demanding art form and attracting the attention of both the public and the media to men's style, a radically innovative concept when he started out. By 1963 a gigantic poster on the Champs-Elysées proclaimed 'S'habiller Smalto' (*Wear Smalto*); four years later the Smalto style was available as ready-to-wear; and two decades of expansion led to the construction of nothing less than a small empire.

Very few other people in the world, except in Italy, have been able to succeed with the dangerous transition between traditional tailoring and luxury ready-to-wear. In the late 1960s Smalto went back to his native Italy to make a careful selection of workshops that would enable him to bring to the market an extremely stylish ready-to-wear line of

The lightest tuxedo in the world was crafted by Francesco Smalto in 1975. It weighs less than 400 grams (14 oz) and is made of *crêpe-de-chine*.

clothing whose considerable success never weakened. He also established a uniquely sophisticated style that sets off the male figure to great advantage, thanks to his particular attention to proportion.

'You Need to Ask for Smalto'

In the late 1950s word spread among the Paris intelligentsia: 'If you go to Camps, you need to ask for Smalto.' Smalto, then head cutter of the firm owned by Joseph Camps, was already one of Paris's most sought-after tailors.

Five years earlier, however, fresh from technical college in Turin, he had literally forced his way into Camps's workshop to beg for a position, even lying about his age (he claimed to be two years older than he was). Even then the young Smalto was far from the mark: 'My cutters are all over fifty,' Camps replied, amused by the ebullient and ambitious young man, 'and I still need to correct them.' Smalto assured the Catalan master that he could reproduce a Camps suit 'just by watching it on the back of someone walking by', and offered to work for nothing for three months as a trial period.

Against all odds, Camps accepted the offer and gave him the cutting table at the back of the workshop to share with two other workers. Smalto was forbidden access to Camps's personal styling workshop (where important secrets were kept), but was assigned his first clients.

At the age of twenty-seven, Smalto became the illustrious firm's fourth cutter. Four years later he had become head cutter, a meteoric rise in the context of a profession where most gained the ultimate title of first cutter only after twenty years of strenuous work. At that time the Camps workshop contained the profession's dream team: Joseph Camps, Henri Urban, Claude Rousseau, Francesco Smalto and also a young *apiéceur* (piece-maker) named Gabriel Gonzalez, who would become a highly esteemed Parisian tailor in his own right (he still works at Cifonelli).

Six years later the insatiably ambitious Smalto, whose name had been buzzing around Paris,

realized that the heyday of bespoke tailoring had come to an end. Refusing to 'spend the rest of his life tailoring suits for the over-privileged', he had the idea of creating a luxury ready-to-wear collection grounded in bespoke culture. After six years studying with Camps, he decided to make a big leap and cross the Atlantic to learn about the new methods of mass production, a booming industry there at the time.

Indeed, while European traditional tailoring was still fighting its last battles in the late 1950s, ready-to-wear was rising to triumph in the United States with its flagship 'sack suit', an easy-to-wear outfit made popular by Ivy League students and such firms as Brooks Brothers on Madison Avenue in New York. It was to give rise to the 'preppy' style, with which the American industry would conquer the world.

Smalto therefore searched for an employer who would teach him the new methods that enabled a suit to be made in three hours rather than the seventy required at the Camps workshop. He would receive the providential help of a rich American client whom he had befriended during fittings at Camps. 'I'll order fifteen suits, but only if they are designed, cut and assembled by Mr Smalto': with that request, the generous customer twisted the arm of the famous H. Harris, President Kennedy's personal tailor, whose workshop was on 57th Street in New York. Harris hired Smalto for three months, enabling him to cross the Atlantic.

In that way, Smalto started out in the United States working for a single customer for three months. That customer went so far as to place another order to give Smalto the time to learn the American techniques – evidence of the special bond Smalto created with his clients.

Throughout his career, many famous people vaunted Smalto's name out of sheer adoration and respect. The singer Charles Aznavour would always start his shows by saying 'I'm dressed by Smalto', and the writer Françoise Sagan said he was 'a real king'.

This Smalto bespoke double-breasted suit displays a quintessentially French silhouette.

This ready-to-wear
Smalto three-piece suit
bears the signature style
of the house: the famous
'Parisian' lapel notch and
a structured shoulder that
is slightly padded and
curved inwards.

A bespoke Smalto
three-piece suit of 1964.

A Star Is Born: The Rise
of Francesco Smalto

In 1962, with the assistance of one Monsieur Landi, a fellow Italian worker whom he had met at Camps's workshop, Smalto started his own tailoring business, hardly ten years after arriving in Paris from Italy to discover the world of men's fashion. From the very beginning, Smalto's collections showed intriguing modernity: 'My goal was to change men, the way people considered men's figures,' he confessed years later.

People were surprised by Smalto's close-fitting suits, with their narrow shoulders and high sleeveheads, which shook up the old ways. He chose lighter linings, flaring jackets and thinner fabrics, and invented the notion of the 'second skin suit', a concept he would pursue obsessively. In 1964 he became the official tailor of King Hassan II of

Morocco, who was subsequently named 'the most elegant man in the world' twice by an Italian magazine.

In 1967 Smalto presented his ready-to-wear collection, made in Italy in his specially selected workshops. The first-rate quality and outstanding style of his suits helped the clothing industry as a whole to make a huge leap forward, since luxury ready-to-wear designed by a famous master tailor was unheard of in Paris.

With the opening of his famous shop in rue François Premier in 1970, Smalto's business really took off, and the world of show business, especially actors, embraced the Smalto style. Jean-Paul Belmondo, then the most popular actor in France, picked Smalto as his official tailor, and even sported the house's emblem, the well-known red carnation. Other major figures

Left to right: Two double-breasted bespoke overcoats (*redingotes*) from 1963 and a contemporary double-breasted overcoat with a fur collar.

Overleaf

This vintage 'second skin' tuxedo made of *crêpe-de-chine* was one of Francesco Smalto's personal specialities in the 1970s.

charge of the signature style for the ready-to-wear department. In 1998–2000 the firm returned with two fashion shows that caused quite a sensation. Put on at a time when French sport was at its best, they featured football players and other top sportsmen as models.

In 2007 Boclet passed the baton to the young Youn Chong Bak, who had started out at Smalto as an intern a few years earlier. She took charge of the style that had made the house internationally famous and with a deft touch helped it to grow even further.

Clear Lines for Men

I cannot imagine a better way to describe Smalto's art than to use an analogy from the art of the comic. It seems to me that Smalto was the suit designer who used a *ligne claire*. This phrase – coined by the Dutch cartoonist and graphic designer Joost Swarte in 1977 during an exhibition devoted to Hergé, the inventor of Tintin – is the perfect description for the Smalto style: clean, neat, direct lines, almost geometric and with a fastidious way of isolating each part of the garment and respecting its proportion. Even ready-to-wear Smalto bears the signature style of the firm: a 90-degree lapel notch and a narrow shoulder, slightly curved inwards, its sleevehead wide and high and with a slight cigarette roll.

Francesco Smalto Couture: The Bespoke Workshop

Even though ready-to-wear has been a major part of the firm's business since the early 1970s, Smalto always made sure that a first-class bespoke workshop producing entirely handmade pieces in keeping with the canons of traditional tailoring remained at its heart. This bespoke workshop, which boasts the custom of many heads of state – not only the king of Morocco – has always worked according to the standards and methods set by its founder.

Following his master, Joseph Camps, Smalto worked for many years to devise his own system for taking measurements and producing templates, as well as organizing work according to a thirty-three-part 'step-by-step' process that trained tailors to specialize in a couple of techniques each. Such a system, which can work only in bespoke houses endowed with many workers, ensures the highest

followed, including Sean Connery, Roger Moore and Jerry Lewis.

In 1973 the brand gained international status as Smalto opened franchise shops in London, Brussels, Tokyo and New York. In 1974 and 1984 he opened two more shops in Paris, on place Victor Hugo and rue Saint-Honoré. Always seeking to innovate, Smalto made a splash in 1975 when he created the lightest dinner jacket on earth, made of silk *crêpe-de-chine* and weighing only 380 grams. It was not just light, however; the fabric still hung with impeccable grace. In 1987 eighteen shops bore the name of the founder, and close to 45,000 ready-to-wear suits made by as many as 170 employees and bearing the Smalto signature were sold globally.

Smalto designed his collections himself until 1991. In 1995 he decided to focus on bespoke tailoring, and put his disciple Franck Boclet in

level of excellence and skill at each step of the production of a garment. This type of organization has been the hallmark of such houses as Huntsman & Sons in London.

By labouring over his research and fine-tuning these techniques for his own workshop, Smalto ensured that his skill, his methods, his vision and the core of his style were all passed on to the new generations of cutters, tailors, piece-makers and breech-makers. In 2012, as if to prove the success of this process of transmission, Smalto's firm received the label 'Entreprise du Patrimoine Vivant', an official distinction from the French state for companies that possess and promote a rare and historic skill.

The Francesco Smalto Couture workshop is now one of the five most important in Paris. In the face of a new interest in men's bespoke tailoring, it has opened up to a younger clientele, with a more cosmopolitan, less exclusive approach. They come to Smalto to find the suits, jackets, waistcoats and coats that stand out among the most beautiful and most refined in the world.

'A Smalto Suit Will Always Look Better'

Beyond Smalto's flair for the finest cut, his genius was to embrace the ready-to-wear revolution and present well-designed and well-made collections when other tailors stuck to their guns, holding on to traditional ideas and ignoring the assault of the mass industry that was flooding the market. Although Smalto's collections evolved through the years, and he was not immune to changing in response to aesthetic trends, he managed to keep his own style alive, making sure his fundamental signature was recognizable even when someone else was in charge – whether the wild child Franck Boclet or the sensual Youn Chong Bak.

When I mentioned to an old friend – a connoisseur of all things sartorial – that I was writing this book, he couldn't help remarking: 'Somehow, a Smalto suit always looks better than other suits.' Perhaps, then, the man who wanted to be crowned the best tailor of his times succeeded in his goal.

Two further examples of Smalto's 'second skin' ultra-light tuxedo.

A luxurious Smalto exotic-skin sports jacket.

BERLUTI ATELIERS ARNYS

The Spirit of the Parisian Left Bank

In 2012, the news that Arnys had been bought by LVMH came as a bolt from the blue for those in the small world of classic elegance. As an independent tailor and house of luxury ready-to-wear, Arnys was bought in order to beef up Berluti's bootmaking offering, thereby creating an all-encompassing new brand for men. I know of several gentlemen who were on the verge of tears when they heard about it, as if they had lost a dear friend and their lives were forever changed.

It is true that Maison Arnys always had a special relationship with its clients, even a unique rapport. The house, which was founded in 1933 by Jankel Grimbert and run by two different generations of the family, managed to carve a radically individual niche within the landscape of high-end clothing for men.

The impact the Grimbert brothers had on Parisian style is reminiscent of that of Olga Berluti on the field of footwear (see page 112) before her business too was bought by LVMH in 1993. Both companies – Berluti and Arnys – had a way of exerting great influence while remaining quiet about it. Both houses wielded this influence thanks to their real sartorial freedom of expression as well as the input of their remarkably faithful customers.

At the time, Charvet was probably the only other house in Paris that could claim the same kind of devoted following, but it was more *bourgeois*, even aristocratic, whereas the Arnys boutique on rue de Sèvres rather appealed to the rebellious figures of Paris's Left Bank. Jean Cocteau, Yves Saint Laurent, Jean-Paul Sartre, Pablo Picasso, Fernando Botero and Orson Welles, among many others, were worshippers of that wonderful boutique, which in November 2013 became Berluti's Paris flagship.

Bernard Arnault of LVMH transformed Berluti and its former owner into icons of contemporary French luxury in the eyes of the whole world, just by bringing to the fore its strong and singular stylistic legacy. One can bet that he will likewise give prominence to the extraordinary legacy of the small Arnys boutique, thanks to his experienced artistic director, Alessandro Sartori (formerly of the Italian brand Zegna), and also thanks to the brand's style heritage, created by the maverick brothers Jean and Michel Grimbert, two genuine gentlemen with perfect taste who have shown great talent for the art of the paradox, managing to turn out collections of extravagant classicism and joyful understatement.

Jackets wait for fittings behind the cutting desk at Berluti's bespoke atelier, on the first floor of its flagship at rue de Sèvres, on Paris's Left Bank.

Family and Brotherhood

Arnys is a small family company founded in Paris by Jankel Grimbert, a Jewish immigrant from Russia. It has always been run by brothers: first Léon and Albert, Jankel's sons, then from 1966 by Michel and Jean Grimbert. Until 1940 it was essentially a Parisian tailor offering bespoke suits, shirts and ties, in common with all luxury tailors of the time.

In 1946, after a period of dormancy for the company during the war, Léon Grimbert visited his family in the United States and discovered the rapidly expanding phenomenon of ready-to-wear, a novelty that was yet unknown in Europe. When he returned to France he and Albert decided to start gradually offering ready-to-wear clothes made in small batches with luxury fabrics, in colours that had hitherto been available only for bespoke.

A significant change occurred when the Grimberts started working with Simon Ackerman, a British entrepreneur who had settled in New York and then returned to set up the famous company Chester Barrie in London in 1935. Arnys became a regular customer of Ackerman, developing with his help a type of 'ready-to-wear tailoring' that was peerless in Paris: fine clothes with a perfect cut and finishings that could be adjusted to the client,

without the price and delay of bespoke tailoring. This British connection also explains how Arnys gradually introduced typically English gentlemen's clothes into its collection, including the celebrated colourful Shetland jumpers. The Arnys style was coming into its own, exemplifying post-war men's style in Saint-Germain-des-Prés better than any other brand.

The Forestière Jacket: The Epitome of Left Bank Elegance

I believe it is perfectly to the point to say that Arnys was the symbol of Left Bank men's style (as was Berluti, in footwear). It is not even media hype. I think the original Berluti boutique on rue Marbeuf in the 1980s already had that special Saint-Germain and Latin Quarter flavour despite its location at the heart of the Right Bank's golden triangle – a fine example of 'anatopism', to use the great novelist Michel Tournier's term for the spatial equivalent of 'anachronism'.

Although the difference has now faded slightly, the contrast between the styles of the Left Bank (supposedly rebellious, turbulent, progressive, intellectual; at first spontaneous, and now just for show) and the Right (conservative, bourgeois,

Karim Rehabi, head cutter, and Alfredo Orlandi, master tailor.

La Forestière, a 'working jacket' created by Léon Grimbert of Arnys for Le Corbusier in 1947. This iconic garment has become, over the years, an emblem of the Left Bank 'casual chic' and gentle rebel style.

classic) was never as sharp as during the early 1950s in the area of Saint-Germain, boulevard Raspail, rue de Sèvres and boulevard du Montparnasse. After the Second World War, Saint-Germain and the Left Bank more generally was where things were happening with great intensity in the fields of philosophy, literature, music and the arts. Menswear followed that trend, and, in the general ambiance of whimsical excess, boldness took precedence over classicism, while nonchalance cancelled out the stiffness of received codes of behaviour.

This was not yet the revolution that followed the violent civil unrest in France in May 1968, but nevertheless jackets were becoming less and less structured, ties were loosened (but certainly not taken off), the young generation worshipped jazz musicians (and with them striped suits) and shoes were taking on vivid two-tone hues.

In such an intense context, stylistic reference points inevitably shifted. The bourgeois classics of the time were replaced by more varied pieces, sometimes quite surprisingly so, with aesthetic nods to the countryside, to the style of artisans and the working class.

At the beginning of that golden Left Bank era, Léon Grimbert, the father of Jean and Michel, designed for Le Corbusier a 'work jacket', the Forestière, that allowed the architect–designer–painter–sculptor to move about in his workshop with unparalleled ease. Wide and slightly off-centre sleeveheads enabled the wearer literally to roll up his sleeves and show a very refined coloured lining.

Léon's inspiration for the garment was the jacket worn by gamekeepers in Sologne (a forested region in north-central France), with patch pockets and a stand-up collar. The new design was in effect a sartorial existentialist statement at a time when rejecting middle-class values was de rigueur among the Left Bank's artistic community, which included such varied people as Boris Vian, Sartre,

Simone de Beauvoir, Juliette Gréco, Jean-Luc Godard, François Truffaut, Jacques Prévert and Alberto Giacometti.

I was fortunate enough to talk at length to the charming Jean Grimbert about that era. We discussed how his family captured so brilliantly the zeitgeist and how they injected their tailoring style with a well-mannered but deliberate disdain for the middle-class conventions that still dominated. That is what made Arnys such a special *maison* in the sartorial landscape of Paris and even the world.

A Colourful Style for Men

Cocteau once famously described the French as 'sad Italians' (or, depending on your source,

At the magnificently renovated Berluti flagship in rue de Sèvres, Parisian gentlemen can dress from head to toe and discover fine pieces of luggage that are among the most elegant and distinctive on the market.

The first floor of Berluti's
Left Bank boutique:
probably one of the
most refined menswear
boutiques in the world.

Overleaf

Three Berluti bespoke
coats, photographed by
Andy Julia at Berluti's
bespoke salon in Paris in
February 2015.

the Italians as 'good-natured Frenchmen').
The Grimbert brothers have tried throughout
the history of their firm to gainsay or soften
that pertinent remark, and to bring a touch of
colour and charm to their take on Parisian style.

Colour has always been a characteristic of
Arnys. The brothers never took the easy path
of solids in their work, preferring to offer Parisian
gentlemen sophisticated and comfortable clothes
with a recognizable touch of colour, be it in the
form of contrasting lapels, vibrant linings or other
finishing details. The boutique on rue de Sèvres
had a great reputation among connoisseurs for its
impressive range of colours in jumpers, shirts, ties,
pocket squares and accessories.

Arnys Berluti's Soft Tailoring

The tailors from Arnys are still at work in the
fabulous Berluti shop on rue de Sèvres. Taking on
the legacy of the Grimbert brothers, Berluti Bespoke
offers soft tailoring of remarkable quality. It is in
line with the legacy of Arnys and the Grimbert
brothers: sophisticated and supple tailoring with
a dash of comfortable casualness.

This is classy tailoring, following traditional
standards. It shows that Berluti intends to protect
and continue the extraordinary contribution
of the Grimbert family to the stylistic debates
that rage among connoisseurs in Paris, throughout
France and the rest of the world. Long live Left
Bank style!

CHEMISIERS
IN
PARIS

In London, Milan, Rome or Naples, small workshops and small businesses specializing in bespoke shirts are still fairly numerous, but in Paris – except for the sacrosanct giant that is Charvet, whose sublime boutique has pride of place on place Vendôme – very few serious shops continue to offer a genuine bespoke shirt service.

I have often said, on my website *Parisian Gentleman* and elsewhere, that such shirts enable young men or gentlemen with limited means, who cannot reach the holy grail of bespoke suits, to enter the esoteric and addictive world of traditional bespoke in a gradual way. The remaining houses that still turn out shirts according to traditional standards are few and far between – barely a handful, actually – but they offer to Parisian aesthetes, and to anyone else who loves fine bespoke clothing, shirts of superb quality, made in France and for prices that are not unreachable. And here I am not talking about the numerous shops that offer 'fake' bespoke, presenting 'computerized' measures (what a paradox!), whose so-called house-made shirts are actually made very far from Paris or even Europe.

In Paris, three small companies who rival one another in understatement are the favourites of elegant Parisians. Lucca, run by Didier Lucca and his mother on the boulevard des Batignolles, is at the forefront. Their fantastic bespoke shirts delight their demanding and loyal clientele.

In similar fashion, but in a more exclusive neighbourhood in the 16th arrondissement, Halary (named after its founder, Patrice Halary) boasts a notably upper-class clientele, mostly businessmen and lawyers. Its shirts are made in Chalon-sur-Saône by Gauthier, the company that also produces shirts for none other than Hermès. Halary's fine traditional shirts offer everything shirt-lovers are fond of, with all the high-end options expected by purists: Australian mother-of-pearl buttons shaped at Corne et Corozo in Lyon, DHJ interlinings (the experts will know about those) and so on. The firm works with specially selected textile companies of great reputation, such as Masons, Söktaş and Alumo.

Located since 1998 at the same address on avenue Victor Hugo, Halary is an expert in the art of detail – and not just in its shirts. The cups in which its customers are served coffee are specially designed

for the company, and even the shirt packages are handmade and come from Bossa Art in Barcelona; they are lined with tissue paper bearing the house logo. Halary also presents a dazzling range of splendid handmade ties by Boivin that tie specialists know very well.

Finally, across the Seine on the Left Bank is Courtot, run by Cydonia Courtot and his wife. This is an address that shirt-lovers will not hesitate to recommend. Cydonia's grandmother, who was born in 1898, learned the trade of shirt-making after selling silk hose. After the First World War she opened a small shirt workshop, for both ready-to-wear and bespoke, in Croissy-sur-Seine, employing up to twenty seamstresses at a time. Her boutique

was then on the Champs-Elysées; her son Edouard bought another shop, at 113 rue de Rennes, in 1962. He started out selling ties, cufflinks, socks and polo shirts, but it wasn't long before he turned back to the speciality his mother had taught him, and he perfected his skill in his lovely boutique-cum-workshop.

Edouard's son Cydonia began his trade very early: while his friends played in the streets, he learned with his father how to cut interlinings for the cuffs of the house shirts. Courtot Shirt-maker now stands proudly among Paris's specialists in beautiful, traditional shirts. The firm makes every possible effort (and that's an understatement) to satisfy its loyal customers, offering each a unique pattern and paying attention to every suggestion with extreme kindness. No wonder the clientele is expanding.

Lucca, Halary and Courtot are three traditional shirt-makers that continue to prosper, for the renewed pleasure of connoisseurs, next to the Parisian icon that is Maison Charvet.

The small, traditional Parisian bespoke shirt-maker Courtot crafts exquisite shirts with purist details.

Cydonia Courtot is pictured in front of his shop on rue de Rennes, on the Left Bank.

CHARVET

Chemisier in Paris

In 1869 the Prince of Wales (later Edward VII) issued a Royal Warrant to Edouard Charvet, making the French house an official supplier to the British Crown. The text bears the name 'Charvet, Chemisier in Paris'. Such a rare use of a French term in an official document issued by the British Crown shows that the future king held the Parisian shirt-maker and his magnificent work in high esteem. It is also testimony to the Charvet family's pioneering role as creators of a new type of business. Shirt-making as such did not exist until Joseph-Christophe 'Christofle' Charvet created it, in 1838. Men would usually have their shirts sewn by their linen maids using fabric supplied by those maids. The patterns were very simple and followed a straight outline, without the slightest inward curve.

In 1838, however, for the first time in history, customers at Charvet's boutique – the 'Chemisier in Paris' – could have their measurements taken, select their fabric and have their shirts made up, all in the same shop. It was a revolution in its way, resulting from the flair of Christofle Charvet, who had guessed the turn men's clothing was taking and anticipated men's budding taste for a tighter fit and for the more ambitious curved outlines, collars and shoulder yokes.

To this day Charvet remains the most famous bespoke shirt-maker in the world, and that with only one own-brand shop: 28 place Vendôme. Its shirts, ties, waistcoats, robes, handkerchiefs and other accessories are worshipped all over the world. Its famous customers have been so numerous since the nineteenth century that it might well be less daunting to list major figures who have *not* patronized the firm. Such towering historical figures as Edward VII, Hector Berlioz, Charles Baudelaire, Marcel Proust, Harry S. Truman, John Fitzgerald Kennedy, Fred Astaire, Claude Monet, Gary Cooper, Pablo Picasso, Charles de Gaulle, Ernest Hemingway, Winston Churchill, Ronald Reagan, Jacques Chirac, François Mitterrand and Barack Obama have all worn its shirts. This, after all, is a firm that invented a whole new type of business, and whose name has been adopted to describe the type of silk it uses to make its incredible ties.

Telling the story of such a Parisian institution is a challenge. Many of the world's great personalities have been in this boutique, and interest has even been taken in its destiny at state level, as we shall see.

A collection of men's fashion illustrations by the French artist Jean Choiselat.

The second floor of Charvet's atelier is dedicated to bespoke shirts: here, formal white shirt samples and eight kinds of cuff are displayed.

Bertrand Fraysse, a French journalist writing for *Challenges* magazine, recently attempted to sum up the history of Charvet by saying, with no little insight, that the *maison* founded in 1838 by Christofle Charvet, the son of Emperor Napoleon I's wardrobe keeper and the cousin of Louise Charvet (Napoleon's butler's wife, and so in charge of the emperor's shirts), stands out today as somewhat anachronistic and abnormal. I will add that Charvet is even more than just economically anachronistic and anomalous: it is a wonderland and an exemplar.

Charvet: A Quaint Anachronism

As the only survivor of the vibrant group of great Parisian shirt-makers from the 1950s (who remembers Bouvin, Poirier, Seelio and Seymous, who have long gone the way of the bison?), Charvet is one of the last emblems of a type of business that died out under pressure from the mechanized clothing industry in the 1960s and 1970s. While it is easy enough today to stock up on a few hundred shirts in a garage, launch an online shop with a 'Made in Italy' logo and claim that one is a 'shirt-maker', Charvet continues to ply its luxury shirt and tie trade the way it always has, following the high standards the firm itself established almost two centuries ago.

Even though Charvet is undeniably a glorious anachronism today, I firmly believe that buying a shirt or tie at Charvet's must always have been something special, an experience outside time. The novelist Marcel Proust loved to spend time there, picking up his shirts, ties and *marcel* vests.[1] He didn't fail to pay tribute to his favourite shirt-maker, mentioning Charvet in his novels, especially in one famous instance, in *A L'Ombre des jeunes filles en fleur* (1918, translated as *Within a Budding Grove*; the second volume of *A La Recherche du temps perdu*, known as *Remembrance of Things Past*), where the narrator 'roams to and fro among the avenues, tightening every few minutes the knot of a gorgeous necktie from Charvet's'.

The poet, playwright and artist Jean Cocteau, meanwhile, considered Charvet to be a magic place 'where rainbows stole their ideas'. And for his candidacy to the Académie Française in 1893, the poet Paul Verlaine chose to be photographed by Otto Wegener with a splendid Charvet scarf given to him by the famous French dandy and poet Robert de Montesquiou, himself a faithful customer of Charvet.

Today, more than ever, paying a visit to Charvet's at least once should be a compulsory part of any young man's sartorial education. At the Charvet boutique – as nowhere else in the world – one can see an incredible array of 6,000 fabrics, always available in full length, which means that one can always try them on. There are 500 types of white fabric and 200 blues, as well as 8,000 ties (5,000 new models every season).

The celebrated shop has always had a unique ambiance. Its customers are plunged, the minute they set foot inside, into a cornucopia of colour and fabric. This flair for lavish display, offering an apparently infinite variety of fabrics and patterns, has from the very beginning been a hallmark of Charvet. As early as the nineteenth century, the firm was recognized for the colourful exuberance of its presentation as well as for the quality of its products. In 1904 a foreign journalist even compared it to a show by Loïe Fuller, the American dancer famous for her multicoloured flounces, which whirled as she danced.

An Anomaly: The Strange Case of Charvet

It is fascinating to ponder how a bespoke shirt- and tie-maker should possibly be able to offer such an abundance of fabrics, such a feast of colours and such a treasure trove of accessories in a single shop – in a day and age when computerization, marketing and strategic planning seem to have taken precedence over the love of beautiful things. Likewise, it seems a mystery how such a company should keep functioning in almost the same way

Clockwise from top left: The facade of Charvet's majestic boutique at 28 place Vendôme, Paris; the famous 'wall of whites', offering more than 500 white fabrics in 100 shades (with 6,000 different fabrics available, Charvet provides the largest variety of fine fabrics in the world); three examples of Charvet collars; exquisite fine shirt fabrics in multicoloured stripes.

Overleaf

More than 8,000 handmade ties are displayed on the legendary ground floor. Charvet develops its own designs and exclusive colours, and launches more than 5,000 new models each year.

[1] The *marcel* does not derive its name from Marcel Proust (nor, as online legend has it, from Marcel Eisenberg, the owner of the Établissements Marcel, nor from the boxing champion Marcel Cerdan). It is simply a man's name – some will say a manly name – that came to designate a piece of clothing worn by men, typically workers who needed to have free movement, before it became standard underwear at the end of the nineteenth century. The *marcel* or *débardeur* is a sleeveless shirt often called a 'vest' in British English and a 'singlet' in Australian English (although the Americans call it an 'A-shirt' or 'tank top', using the term 'vest' to describe a waistcoat). Strangely enough, in American English a *marcel* is a hairstyle, typical of the Jazz Age (although the word was first used in 1895), with a deep wave made by using a heated curling iron. It is named after the French hairdresser François Marcel Grateau.

as it has for the past 180 years, regally ignoring advertising and with only one apparent strategy: to offer the best possible products.

In fact, Charvet's secret is hardly a puzzle at all. It's even blatant to anyone who crosses the threshold of 28 place Vendôme: the firm's single obsession is the products it offers. It looks very much as though, over the generations, Charvet has only ever cared about its timeless mission to produce the most beautiful products in the world of shirts and ties. It appears never to have lost that focus, and *actually* to have made the most beautiful shirts, ties and accessories available on the global market.

Now that the trend among consumers (particularly among gentlemen all over the world) seems to be drifting back towards high-quality products rather than brand names, Charvet might well be, once again, at the vanguard of modernity, as was often the case in the past. Through thick and thin, the firm has never sacrificed quality, and now that it offers an unprecedented range of patterns, fabrics and models, it stands as the quintessential Parisian luxury house. The name Charvet is a benchmark thanks to the sheer quality of its products and the richness of its 180-year history.

Charvet is indeed an anomaly; its longevity is not in line with any economic model or rationale. Long-winded economic statistics could probably explain its worldwide glory, but for me the explanation lies in an intangible factor, something that only a very few truly great establishments can offer.

There is indeed something of a metaphysical dimension to it, as the French writer Gilles Lipovetsky tried to explain in an interview with the philosopher Pierre-Henri Tavoillot about the former's essay *Le luxe éternel* (2003), unconsciously describing the relationship Charvet's customers have with their favourite supplier:

> Throughout history luxury has had an intrinsic relation with time. Patrons in antiquity would spend fortunes for their memory to be celebrated. Today, luxury brands are doing the same thing, albeit in a paradoxical form. On the one hand, innovation is a compulsory factor and follows the logic of fashion, of being in the present time. But on the other hand, they also need to harp on their founding myths and on their legendary past, tradition and ancestral craftsmanship. On the consumer's side, the same ambivalence is played out – one should be trendy but also enjoy something with a timeless appeal. A luxury item is not to be consumed haphazardly. The rituals are part of the enjoyment: one buys and loves things for the weight of time, memory and eternity that they carry. In our disposable society, luxury makes you feel the depth of time and brings an element of timelessness that denies death. Paradoxically, there is something very spiritual at the heart of materialistic passions.'

Nicholas Foulkes was also aiming at this idea when he wrote in the *Financial Times* that Charvet was 'a spiritual order that masquerades as a shirt-maker' (13 July 2013).

The master tailor works in Charvet's tailoring salon on the fifth floor.

A vintage weight is engraved with the name of the house.

All Charvet ties are strictly made by hand.

The seriousness of the approach to the art of shirt-making at Charvet cannot be overstated, given the firm's obsession with the tiniest detail. Whether ready-to-wear, by special order or made-to-measure, each shirt is hand-stitched by a single person in the workshop in Saint-Gaultier in the Indre region of central France, where Charvet's factory employs fifty seamstresses. Each shirt shows extreme, obsessive attention to such details as the precision of evenly spaced stitches and the symmetry of patterns at the seams.

The ability to seam patterns on every part of the shirt is indeed a sign for any connoisseur of Charvet shirts: the perfect joining of the placket and the front, of the outside and inside collar, of the back and the sleeves with the one-piece yoke, and even of the sleeve and the sleeve placket. On top of that, the thread used for the buttonholes will always match the main stripe of the fabric.

The rest of the details are in the same spirit. The collars are neat but without stiffness, as they are built with five layers of fabric that are not glued together. There is a double row of single-needle stitches, made separately. Not sparing the amount of fabric needed, the sides are cut straight for neatness of shape and for comfort. The left cuff of the shirt is always slightly larger (even in the ready-to-wear version) to accommodate a watch. Such consideration and exquisite detail represent a wonderland for shirt-lovers.

The house ties are the Everest of their kind. They are responsible for the adoption of the term *soie Charvet* (Charvet silk) to describe the fabric of peerless weight and texture that is used for most of the firm's ties. The ties are all handmade, using exclusive patterns and colours (between 5,000 and 8,000 models come out every year), and unique trade secrets, such as the hidden colour used for every pattern to give greater depth and shimmer to each tie.

Charvet: A National Treasure

In 1965 Denis Colban, then one of Charvet's main suppliers, was informed by Charles de Gaulle's Ministry for Industry that the general had been worried to hear that the heirs of his favourite shirt-maker (and that of numerous other heads of state) were planning to sell the business to American investors. Indeed, Charvet had been on the Americans' radar for some time, being among

The Charvet Wonderland

Almost from the off, Charvet was celebrated around the world for its astounding shirts and ties, and the high quality of its products was acknowledged unanimously. The firm thus gained entry into the closed circle of undisputed luxury names whose mere mention makes one bow in respect. What makes Charvet's shirts and ties so special – and the reason so many gentlemen bother to travel the world to have their shirts made there, when there are many excellent boutiques in Italy and Great Britain – is that Charvet gives them something they will never find elsewhere: an almost limitless choice and the guarantee that their shirt, tie, handkerchief, waistcoat, robe or pyjamas will be made according to the highest standards of traditional shirt-making.

the first Parisian luxury houses to cross the Atlantic. As early as 1853, its ready-to-wear shirts were being exported to the United States, where they enjoyed an excellent reputation. It is entirely possible that Charvet's success was at the root of the creation, at the end of the nineteenth century, of such great American shirt- and tie-makers as the cult Sulka in New York and Chicago, which was clearly trying to compete with Charvet in a field the French firm had quite literally invented.

In 1965, however, Colban – an astute businessman and accomplished display artist – decided to buy Charvet himself. Things were far from rosy: mass-produced ready-to-wear clothing was taking over the whole sector, and Parisian tailors and shirt-makers were closing one after the other. Standardization, large-scale production and the new advertising concept of 'value-for-money' reigned supreme. Without converting to mass production and discount prices, houses like Charvet seemed doomed. The handover was a turning point for the company, however, which under Colban's leadership would withstand not only the crisis triggered by pressure from mass ready-to-wear suppliers but also the tempests of fashion and trend, and emerge stronger, ready for a new era of success and expansion. Colban not only saved Charvet but also developed the business in a climate particularly unfriendly to traditional makers, whose economic model and prices were considered antiquated.

As most firms chose to downgrade their production, Colban chose to upgrade his. Instead of yielding to the far more profitable temptation of selling out and adopting industrial production, he chose to act as the keeper of the flame and protect the name of his business. He pushed the Charvet envelope by offering more choice and more models across his range.

In 1982, after moving from 25 to 8 place Vendôme, Charvet moved into its new quarters at number 28. Colban transformed the new shop into a shrine for connoisseurs from all over the world, making it one of the most beautiful luxury boutiques anywhere. Against all odds, he also kept alive the firm's craftsmanship and legendary standards with the renowned label 'Charvet Place Vendôme', and established it definitively as a luxury icon.

That is why I consider Denis Colban, who died in 1994, to be a great and underrated figure of the Parisian world of men's style. The way he secured the continuity of a legendary institution of the calibre of Charvet and enabled it to continue to thrive deserves respect and ought to be acknowledged. It is thanks to Colban and his family that Charvet is still Charvet.

Today, Colban's children Jean-Claude and Anne-Marie run the house with the same concern for quality and excellence and a matching respect for family craftsmanship. When Jean-Claude talks about his business, he seems to be talking about his own family. Colban is about Charvet as much as Charvet is about Colban, as if the history of the two families had become intertwined over time, regardless of the marketing poses and made-up family sagas to which other firms succumb. The history of Charvet is indeed about two families, not one; families who, through generations and beyond blood ties, have shared and defended the same ideals. It represents a remarkable feat rarely matched among luxury firms, except maybe John Lobb's commendable relationship with the Hermès group in the mid-1970s.

The incredible thing about Charvet is that this family feeling seems to extend to the illustrious patrons themselves, who over the years not only extolled the firm's virtues but also declared eternal devotion to Charvet. And when one looks at the long list of historical figures who chose Charvet as their favoured supplier of shirts and ties, from Edward VII to Winston Churchill, one realizes that Charvet is, indeed, woven into the silken fabric of history.

Denis Colban's idea was to offer a luxurious, opulent venue with a level of lavishness and variety that had never been seen before.

OF
SHOES
&
MEN

3

Page 88

The sculpted Belphegor
bespoke shoe by
Pierre Corthay.

The sole of a vintage
Aubercy shoe.

Tokyo, 1 June 2012. I am sitting in the darkness of a cinema. I am slightly nervous. The credits of my film, La Beauté du geste, start rolling.

The Cinemart is a pleasant venue, an arts cinema nestled in a small street of the boisterous Roppongi Minato-Ku neighbourhood. Tonight, the house is full.

As the first image pops up in the dark, a latecomer is lost in the central aisle, looking for a seat. I take his arm and offer him my seat; after all, it's more important that *he* should be comfortable for the screening of a film whose every shot and word I know, and of whose every defect I am painfully aware. I end up sitting on the steps of the auditorium, thinking that if people should doze off, I could at least sneak outside and spare myself the agony of their boredom. I am also terribly nervous about the subtitles. Is the master bootmaker Pierre Corthay's thirty-three-minute monologue really palatable for a Japanese audience who will be forced to read it? Is there anyone here who is actually excited by my stories about great artisans and bespoke shoes?

Ten minutes later I muster the courage to look around me and study the faces I can make out in the dark. I am surprised to see that people are wide awake, with respectful smiles and even moist eyes when Corthay tells of his years of training with his old master.

This is a simple film in which a French bootmaker, a master with an international reputation, explains what his work is about and discovers other incredible workshops belonging to traditional artisans. It has been screened in Paris, London, Tokyo, Dubai and Hong Kong to full houses, audiences who were moved and excited. Perhaps, I think, this is a sign that men care about their shoes.

John Lobb and Berluti

At the dawn of the 1980s, the situation in Paris was very different. Men did not seem very passionate about their shoes, apart from a select few who had had some education on the subject of bespoke footwear, often thanks to their (rich) families. To indulge their passion they would go secretly to the rue Boissy d'Anglas (John Lobb) or rue Marbeuf (Berluti).

The market in Paris at the time could be easily described: at the top was the John Lobb workshop, present in Paris since 1902 and responsible for training almost all the great contemporary bootmakers; now the flagship of the Hermès group, dominant and boasting a rich and faithful clientele of distinguished customers with a clearly anglophile taste (at least when it came to shoes). Berluti was the first bespoke bootmaker to offer luxury ready-to-wear, which it did as early as 1959. This very special house came to embody the renewal of men's shoes in Paris, displaying in the famous window of its shop in rue Marbeuf bold shapes that had generations of penniless would-be sophisticates staring open-mouthed – including yours truly.

John Lobb having launched its beautiful ready-to-wear collection in 1982 (made in Northampton, of course), the situation was clear-cut: Lobb and Berluti shared the Parisian market for luxury shoes. The customers of the former were from the upper-class *bourgeoisie*, quiet anglophiles from upscale neighbourhoods. The latter firm catered for intellectuals and artists with a slightly wilder frame of mind in the spirit of the Left Bank (even if the shop itself was on the other side of the Seine). Apart from

these two, only very small, secret houses in Paris offered luxury shoes, such as Aubercy's remarkable boutique on rue Vivenne (founded in 1935).

Are You for J. M. Weston or Church's?

A slight cut below these firms, two other companies were vying for a much larger market, that of classic high-quality shoes: the French house J. M. Weston from Limoges and the British firm Church's, originally from the St James district of Northampton, the Mecca of British shoemaking.

In the mid-1980s a heated debate pitted the staunch advocates of Weston's 180 loafer against the champions of Church's Grafton. The Weston side praised the 'hunting' or the triple-soled derby, and Church's supporters extolled the tasselled loafer. There was great discord on the boards of the big companies in La Défense, Paris's business quarter. You could observe two enemy clans: the 'nationalists' (for Weston) and the 'traitors', who loved Church's.

Such 'discussions' were to give rise, twenty years later, to the first online forums dedicated to shoes, those mysterious objects of male desire.

As for me, although I was officially among the Westonians – parading my only pair of city derbies as a student after saving my pennies for longer than I care to admit – I had avoided the problem of which maker to side with by buying a magnificent second-hand pair of Church's golden-brown Graftons. I can confess now that wearing them, I felt invincible.

The competition lasted until the end of the 1990s, when the Prada group bought Church's and steered the brand into more showy territory. The rivalry, however, was the backdrop for the rise of a new mid-range market, with brands such as Bowen copying models from the two benchmark houses. In addition, two French firms with a more casual style were about to find their own clientele of customers concerned more with solid than with well-designed shoes: Heschung and Paraboot.

Two beautiful models – a monk strap and an ankle boot – by the young French house Caulaincourt.

J. M. Weston's two most iconic models: the 180 loafer (in brown and black) and the Chasse handmade derby, probably one of the sturdiest shoes in the world.

A rack of beautiful shoes with creative patinas in the workshop of Altan Bottier in Paris.

'I Imagine You Mean Soulier, Monsieur, Not Chaussure?'

In the early 1990s the market changed radically, driven by the energy of Olga Berluti, who transformed men's shoes from purely functional items of clothing into objects of desire. She brought back the dated term *soulier* to indicate the difference between luxury shoes and the more common *chaussures*. This term that had almost fallen out of use was suddenly becoming the rallying cry for a new generation of lovers of luxury footwear, devotees who (including myself) never failed to correct anyone who dared publicly to use the awful word *chaussure* instead. Even if using such an old-fashioned word was only a whimsical and snobbish impulse, it did have an impact, and what may seem a tiny linguistic detail has become a telltale sign of the difference between a mass-produced commodity for consumers who do not care about what they wear, and a luxury article selected by knowledgeable gentlemen.

Replicating the Patina of Time

As her shop in the rue Marbeuf had become the hub of Paris's business and media elite, Olga Berluti had invented a concept that became instantly popular: patina. It was another linguistic shift, and no small revolution: whereas 'patina' had previously been used to describe the natural colours bestowed by the passing of years, it now characterized a method of giving leather a special colour that resembled the patina of time, so as to give the shoe unique character.

The artifice spread. Although it is still seen as anathema by some purists from the rue de Mogador (John Lobb) or from Limoges (J. M. Weston), it gave birth in the early twenty-first century to an altogether new business: the shoe-shining salon.

Of course, a single factor cannot possibly account for the dynamic trend of men's shoes during the last decade. Yet the keen interest in the patinas from rue Marbeuf is the sign of a deeper transformation. All of a sudden, the epitome of the functional item has become not simply a luxury object but a field of expression for a new generation of artisans and artists. Some of the bolder artists have gained public recognition, such as Hom Nguyen, whose imprint of a verse from Baudelaire's *Les Fleurs du Mal* (*Flowers of Evil*) on a pair of Berlutis stands out as a lasting achievement. Other experts,

such as Paulus Bolten in Paris, have even organized 'patina nights' at which shoe enthusiasts are trained in the art of shoe-shining and oxford-pampering.

From about 2005 onwards, Europe's shoemakers (apart from the British firms, whose orthodox ideas and cult of low-key moderation forbid the vulgarity inherent in imitating the patina of time) delved into the business of made-to-order patina, and more generally that of customized shoes. In France, J. M. Weston was (and still is, by the way) the only firm to resist the trend, preferring to focus on high-quality leather and the beauty of its natural patina.

In Paris, some fine houses specialized in customizing men's shoes and offering particularly daring patinas, thereby garnering a local and sometimes international reputation. Altan Bottier – a fine, traditional workshop famous for its 'ready-to-customize' shoes – is such a firm. Its signature model is a superb Adelaide oxford, the ideal candidate for the complex art of patina. The same could be said of the shoes designed by Marc Guyot, who has been revisiting the golden age of men's style for years, developing his own approach through a line of characterful shoes with patina on demand. I must also mention the excellent patina and design work of Caulaincourt, a young house whose reputation is on the rise in Paris thanks to the energetic leadership of its founder, Alexis Lafont.

Paul 'Paulus' Bolten colours a leather hat in his tiny Parisian workshop. Bolten is a great figure in the Parisian 'patina' world and an indisputable shoe-shine artist.

Bolten's coloration work on two different kinds of shoe: a green loafer and a multi-shade brown oxford.

Pierre Corthay and Anthony Delos

The bootmakers Pierre Corthay and Anthony Delos are the French heroes of the luxury shoe revolution that is also taking place in London (with the work of Tony Gaziano and Dean Girling), Budapest (László Vass), Milan (Riccardo Freccia Bestetti) and Tokyo (Koji Suzuki). Corthay is a *Compagnon du Devoir* and *Maître d'Art* (a distinction awarded by the Ministry of Culture, recognizing the artisan and his skill as belonging to the country's 'intangible cultural heritage'). Delos, meanwhile, is a *Compagnon du Devoir*, an orthopaedic specialist and a *Meilleur Ouvrier de France, a prestigious designation that distinguishes the country's most renowned craftsmen in fields as diverse as pastry-making, butchery and tapestry.*

Like many French bootmakers, both men trained in the John Lobb workshop – the finest bespoke bootmaker in the world, according to all connoisseurs. Corthay went on to manage the Berluti

workshop before opening his own bespoke firm in 1990. His younger brother, Christophe – himself also a Compagnon du Devoir – soon joined him. Maison Corthay grew impressively, offering ready-to-wear shoes with the boldest, neatest shapes and designs ever seen on the market. The Corthay brothers even opened a factory in the suburbs of Paris so as to produce shoes 'made in France' that are among the most beautiful in the world. Helped by the arrival of a new partner in 2010, the workshop was propelled to the international forefront of men's shoes.

Anthony Delos, who is ten years younger than Corthay, followed a more gradual path, but has also emerged as one of the heroes of the French shoe renaissance. After supplementing his apprenticeship with a degree in orthopaedics, he set up shop near Saumur in western France, home of the Cavaliers du Cadre Noir (the French military riding academy).

His small workshop, far from the madding Parisian crowd, has built an international reputation among shoe-lovers – often referred to as 'calceophiles'. Finally, in 2012 Delos joined Berluti's bespoke workshop.

These parallel trajectories show just how dynamic the market is for men's shoes in France. It is telling that artisans with a traditional background have been able to garner international applause for the sheer excellence of their craft and the inventive elegance of their products.

France: In the Top Tier of Men's Luxury Shoes

British shoemaking benefits greatly from the nurturing and promotion of particular skills and of a positive image, especially in Northampton, the historical cradle of such factories as Church's, Trickers and Crockett & Jones. However, despite lacking the international recognition enjoyed in the field by Britain, France is among the great bootmaking countries.

Since about 2005 the market has fragmented, and a variety of very competitive new players have come not from the expected places – England or Italy – but rather from Portugal (Carlos Santos), Romania (Saint Crispin's), Hungary (László Vass) and, most notably, Spain (Carmina). Faced with that growing and increasingly competitive global market, French shoemakers are doing well, thanks to time-honoured houses with an international reputation (John Lobb and Berluti), younger firms with an expanding renown (Corthay) and less conspicuous workshops, such as Aubercy – probably the best-kept secret of men's shoemaking – whose jewel of a boutique is highly esteemed by the cognoscenti. As for J. M. Weston, this superb firm has been such a driving force for the whole market that it stands in a category of its own. It is the only shoemaker in the world to own two traditional tanneries,

near Limoges, one dedicated to soles and the other to the more refined task of producing leather for uppers.

Paris: A Proud Capital of Bespoke Shoes

France's capital city has long been in the vanguard of bespoke bootmaking internationally, thanks in great measure to the British crown jewel John Lobb and thus to the Hermès group, of which it became part – in an operation that was managed remarkably well – in 1976. Interestingly enough, John Lobb already had a pronounced Parisian accent, given that its workshop had been in the rue du Faubourg Saint-Honoré since 1902, staffed by French bootmakers working under the British flag.

John Lobb's bespoke *salon*, on the rue de Mogador, is undeniably one of the most beautiful workshops in the world. This unique workshop, which has trained the best boot-, last- and pattern-makers in France (and, indeed, globally), is the ultimate reference for bespoke boots, a highly specialized and demanding art form that very few houses can really master.

Berluti was acquired by the LVMH group in 1993, and has also been able to keep its splendid bespoke workshop, and even expand it handsomely. It remains an international hallmark of bootmaking. Its recruitment of Anthony Delos in 2012 bodes well for the future of the workshop, where unique shoes are still made according to high-quality traditional standards.

Two other workshops, much lauded by connoisseurs, are an essential addition to these famous firms: the Corthay workshop, which boasts no fewer than three Compagnons du Devoir and produces the most marvellously sophisticated shoes, and the bootmaker Dimitri Gomez. Gomez, who works in the Crockett & Jones boutique in Paris, also makes traditional shoes that have garnered him international praise.

JOHN LOBB

The Gospel According to Lobb

In the mid-1970s, just as sartorial trends were going through a revolution and mass-produced ready-to-wear was becoming the norm, John Lobb, the famous British bespoke bootmaker, decided to focus on its traditional bespoke operation in London and let go of its workshop in Paris, at 47 rue du Faubourg Saint-Honoré, which had been inaugurated in 1902.

The Hermès family (some of whose members were personal clients of the workshop) decided in 1976 to buy it, and worked out a global deal with the Lobb family. The brand would be the property of the Hermès group in the whole world *except* the United Kingdom, where it remained the property of the Lobb family and its heirs, who wished to carry on the family business but only on a local scale. In fact, the deal between the two families covered only the Paris bespoke workshop, since the Lobb family had never been involved in ready-to-wear.

When Hermès took over this seventy-four-year-old workshop, it also took on the Parisian bootmakers who worked there. It was thanks to this single workshop that Hermès gradually built up the John Lobb brand. By the time it created its ready-to-wear collection in 1982, Lobb under Hermès was on its way to becoming the most famous luxury brand

for men's shoes in the world. When we take stock of what has been accomplished by the Hermès group in terms of preserving and developing Lobb's bespoke workshop, it is obvious that the agreement of 1976 was a blessing for *both* parties.

Many shoe-lovers must have asked themselves who and where the 'real' John Lobb is. I'm glad to have the opportunity to answer that question. The answer is crystal-clear: John Lobb is Hermès, except in the United Kingdom.

There is also the vexed question, often debated by shoe buffs, of whether the London and Paris bespoke workshops are equal in terms of craftsmanship and respect of tradition. The answer, again, is very simple: yes, they are. It was the same company and the same methods that gave rise to the

The bootmakers of John Lobb are photographed outside the firm's boutique at 47 rue du Faubourg Saint-Honoré, Paris, in about 1960.

The art of making equestrian boots is one of the most demanding in terms of craftsmanship. Only a few ateliers in the world are still practising this art at its highest level, and John Lobb in Paris is among the best.

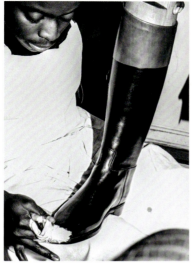

Fifteen highly skilled
craftsmen work in the
John Lobb atelier in Paris.

A bootmaker works on
a bespoke shoe at John
Lobb's workshop on rue
de Mogador. An average
of fifty hours is necessary
to produce a bespoke pair
of shoes according to
the tenets of traditional
shoemaking.

Overleaf

John Lobb's hunting
and riding boots
are breathtaking.

two workshops, in London in 1876 and in Paris in 1902. That kinship ensured that both faithfully kept alive the exceptional legacy of the Lobb family, and both are now rightly considered to be world-famous institutions for bespoke shoes.

The main, and very important, difference is that the shoes made in London comply strictly with British tradition, displaying very conservative lasts and models, whereas the Paris workshop – while never betraying its British legacy – has developed a more sophisticated, daring and up-to-date approach to shoemaking. In other words, a Parisian approach.

One of the Most Beautiful Workshops in the World

I don't think anyone interested in men's bespoke shoes afforded the privilege of visiting the John Lobb workshop in rue de Mogador would argue that it is *the* ultimate workshop. It is the culmination, the summit of bespoke boots and shoes, the be-all and end-all of bootmaking. Most great French bootmakers – including Pierre Corthay and Anthony Delos – were trained there, learning their trade from such famed masters as 'Monsieur Louis' Portella or, more recently, Philippe Atienza.

First located at 47 rue du Faubourg Saint-Honoré, then at number 24 (on the first floor, next to the office of former Hermès president Jean-Louis Dumas) in 1976, the workshop moved for a very short time to a mezzanine in rue des Martyrs and then to rue du Faubourg Saint-Antoine, an area traditional

for its wood craftsmen. In 2009 it was eventually relocated to rue de Mogador, in the headquarters building, next to the CEO's office and the fitting room – at the very heart of the John Lobb company.

The workshop is now a role model, having received the prestigious designation Entreprise du Patrimoine Vivant (Living Heritage Company). It brings together all the complex specialities and crafts of bespoke bootmaking – last-makers and pattern-cutters, clickers and closers – in an exhibition of living heritage.

The shoes are made by a dream team of artisans, two of whom hold the prestigious Meilleur Ouvrier de France title, while another wears the inconspicuous lapel badge of a Chevalier des Arts et Lettres, an official and much prized award given by the French Republic to its most distinguished ambassadors of national culture. Fifteen top craftsmen work in this quiet, elegant place to maintain the glorious spirit of traditional bootmaking.

'Tradition' has become a buzzword of contemporary marketing, so much so that its excessive and hypocritical use by companies looking for those elusive roots has made it something of an empty vessel. The John Lobb workshop is a welcome exception: not only are the artisans' technical processes the same as those performed by their forebears 150 years ago, but also there is no intention of changing them. At John Lobb, tradition is no trifling matter, and the only real rule applied there is one of respect for that legacy.

The Gospel According to Lobb

At John Lobb's, making a pair of bespoke shoes or boots is a complex, time-tested process involving an extraordinary number of different skills and fine technical gestures. As soon as the foot is measured, a table of proportions enables the last-maker to 'interpret' its shape. 'Interpret' is not a word I use lightly: the hornbeam-wood last must be as close as possible to the shape and proportion of the foot, which is felt and studied, bearing in mind the model of shoe chosen by the client, as well as the house style. It is not a simple thing, but the in-house last-makers have perfectly mastered their craft.

It goes without saying that a prototype or 'mock-up' of the shoe is used, so that the bootmaker can refine the fit before the final stages of manufacturing are begun. The leather is left to rest after each stage of the handmaking process. The same care is applied to each of the hundreds of steps – each in line with the standards of traditional bootmaking – that are necessary to produce a bespoke pair of John Lobb shoes. Since no concession is made, it is essential that the maker take time. Such a philosophy is an enchantment.

The whole process for a handmade pair of John Lobb shoes cannot take less than forty hours, and is often closer to sixty. Boots, however – whether country, hunting or riding – are a much greater challenge; they are a John Lobb speciality, but take at least twenty hours longer than the shoemaking process.

The William Flagship

In 1982, six years after purchasing the John Lobb bespoke workshop in Paris, the Hermès group launched a line of ready-to-wear shoes so as to expand the brand's reach and make it accessible to a wider section of elegant gentlemen. As the birthplace of men's shoes, Northampton was the obvious choice for the production of this new line, and the renowned workshop of Edward Green, which would later be described as 'the last bridge between ready-to-wear and bespoke shoemaking', was chosen. Hermès eventually bought this remarkable workshop, in 1994.

To manage such a delicate transition between ready-to-wear and bespoke, Hermès made a deft move, betting with far-sightedness on a model that had been designed as a bespoke shoe in 1945: the illustrious double-buckle monk-shoe called William. Named after William Lobb (who died young, in 1916), this shoe played a major part in the contemporary development of the brand and eventually became for many connoisseurs, including yours truly, the archetypal Lobb shoe.

I remember very well how Paris was suddenly invaded by those dapper double-buckles. I had just managed to buy my first second-hand pair of Church's after much effort (a pair of Grafton derbys), and one of my friends – whose father had been a long-time client of Lobb's – barged in one night with those double buckles that were the talk of the town. I confess my Church's and I were devastated.

Before a pair of bespoke shoes can be made, John Lobb's last-makers use a table of proportions in order to reproduce the customer's unique foot as closely as possible.

A pair of bespoke oxfords with side eyelets is ready to be delivered.

Using the William as the first ready-to-wear model was a stroke of genius. As a classic with a twist (a derby with a double buckle) it was an immediate success, and established John Lobb as a top player for connoisseurs as well as the lay world. Since then it has been copied many times by hundreds of brands, and the double-buckled monk shoe has become a classic in its own right, as the oxford and the derby did before it.

The John Lobb Style

It is often said that there is no artistic director in that workshop. Rather, it is the clients whose orders have helped to define the development of the John Lobb style over the years, gradually adding their own touches and eventually lending a specific identity even to the ready-to-wear collection. Having studied the subject in depth, I can venture to say that the John Lobb style does exist. This deft and delicate fusion of British roots and Parisian sensibility has emerged over the years, bringing refinement, elegance and sophistication to the whole catalogue.

For instance, whether bespoke or ready-to-wear, John Lobb's oxfords are indisputably genuine British oxfords, adorned with perforations, brogueing and wingtips or traditional toecaps. And yet they are unlike any others. They're smoother and more graceful, and bring a more perfectly balanced proportion to the delineation of the leg than do the purely British models. The Saunton model, a classic, sophisticated shoe with utterly perfect proportions, the Becketts, a contemporary geometric design with a softly squared tip, and the Philip II, formal and severe with a Hungarian tip (Budapester) and rounded soles, are all evidence of the slow aesthetic transformation of a brand that has managed to build an international identity without ever forgetting its roots.

The Lobb style is the essence of a glorious stylistic paradox that one may call a sort of creative conservatism, or conservative creativity. It is the result of a unique blending of the sophistication of the Paris touch and the understatement of the London spirit.

The Finest Leather for your Boots

It is the quality of leather used at John Lobb's that separates this house from all other shoemakers. There is no equivalent anywhere for quality and range of hide. Of course, the clout of Hermès in the field of luxury leather is a major asset, and that is how John Lobb can offer leather of outstanding and unequalled quality, as well as hides that cannot be found anywhere else, including exotic skins.

Most leather types are mass-dyed, which means that the colour is soaked deep into the skin in the early stages of tanning, and not just dabbed on to the surface. The resulting colours are deep and subtle, ready to receive the radiant patina of time — for no artificial substitute is accepted at John Lobb's. The market for patina has developed greatly, but John Lobb has stuck to its classic guns and remained steadfastly traditional, although the firm does provide a made-to-order service catering to the customer's choice of colour. After all, a house that already offers the most incredible choice of mass-dyed leather in the world really does not need to offer patina.

Hermès Leather and John Lobb's Welts

The welt, that small strip of leather lining the shoe that enables the bootmaker to connect the upper and the sole, is a peculiar object that requires a very specific know-how. Bootmakers, as well as equestrian saddlers and harness-makers, use a welt to stitch two strips of thick leather together.

For shoe lovers, that small strip sandwiched between two pieces of leather represents sturdiness and durability. It can be seen as the natural symbol linking Hermès and John Lobb — a link that gave birth to the most famous bootmaker in the world, a role model that has played a great part in the preservation of ancient techniques. In the hands of Hermès, John Lobb is still a monument of bootmaking, keeping the tradition alive.

Two John Lobb ready-to-wear shoes and a bespoke buttoned Balmoral boot.

BERLUTI

The Soul of a Shoe

Not many people can claim to have revolutionized a whole industry, but Olga Berluti is one of them. During the 1980s the going was smooth for her exclusive boutique in the rue Marbeuf, the polite and muted hub of artists, politicians and intellectuals. But wild Olga decided to overthrow the rigid codes of a very conservative – and slightly boring – market. Just as Berluti was getting a lot of attention outside Parisian circles for its exquisite ready-to-wear collections, she came up with a radically new concept, giving new meaning to an old word: patina. Everybody took note.

I remember in the mid-1980s window-shopping dreamily on rue Marbeuf (on quiet Sunday afternoons – it's less embarrassing), hypnotized by the Alessandro one-cut shoe, with its wood-like patina, or by a shimmering, reflective olive-green Warhol-inspired Andy loafer. 'Your shoes got soul', said the poster at the back of the splendid window, from the darkness of that special boutique, always reminiscent more of the smoking room of a gentleman's club than of a shoe shop.

At the time John Lobb reigned supreme over high-end and bespoke shoes, while J. M. Weston and Church's, at a slightly lower level, were engaged in fierce and divisive competition, as we have seen. Olga Berluti chose to turn all these codes upside-down, in terms of both consumer habits and style, and introduced a healthy dose of creativity, chutzpah and freedom.

From the very beginning, Berluti's motto has been to do things differently, and that includes carefully choosing its words. At 26 rue Marbeuf, Berluti operates not a shop, but a *salon*. It's not about shoes, either, but about *souliers*. Its employees even teach their distinguished customers how to lace their shoes the way the Duke of Windsor taught Olga – according to company legend.

It is also impossible to fulfil your desires immediately at Berluti's: it just isn't done. Shoes are chosen and sold in the form of raw leather, and so choosing a colour and a type of patina is part and parcel of buying your *souliers*. This stroke of genius means that customers are asked to come back another day – which can only be conducive to new cravings – and makes every one feel that he is buying something unique, customized, meticulously prepared for him alone. Such a concept represents a masterful transfer of the bespoke bootmaking spirit to ready-to-wear footwear, and is surely one of the keys to Berluti's success.

The Alessandro whole-cut shoe, created in 1894 by the eponymous founder, remains Berluti's iconic model and one of the most famous men's shoes in the world.

Madame Berluti's ability to elevate with glamorous poetry what had hitherto been a banal purchase, often influenced by men's wives, put Berluti on the shoe-industry map. It helped to recruit an army of dedicated gentlemen ready to regard Berluti as an informal gentleman's club, not just a boutique – another stroke of genius.

Three decades before the concept of 'social networking' had invaded – even saturated – our lives, Olga Berluti created the first men's club in a shoe shop. She even held special nights that have become part of the legend of Paris's high society: the famous annual meetings of the exclusive and influential Club Swann, incorporating the business, political, artistic and intellectual elite united by the art of shoe-shining and the fondness of men for their shoes. In the 1990s rumours and fantastic tales of these evenings ran wild. Legend has it that these secret polishing meetings always culminated with a few drops of champagne (preferably Dom Pérignon) applied as a glaze before the shoes were presented to the shimmering light of the full moon.

But all that is neither here nor there. The main thing is that Berluti was the first bootmaker to enable some of France's top executives to play like children. Olga persuaded members of the upper crust to gather once a year and sit shoe-less at the table of an award-winning restaurant, like kids at boarding school or on summer camp, and spit cheerfully on their shoes. This gave them the sweet impression of belonging to a tradition of distinguished behaviour epitomized by the character of Charles Swann in the work of Marcel Proust – a fine, cultured man, a true connoisseur of literature and the arts, someone who never boasts or becomes subsumed by the world around him. Such a character was, as Proust puts it in chapter three of *Swann's Way*, the opposite of those '"boring people" who were to be avoided like the plague, and only asked to the big evenings, which were given as seldom as possible, and then only if it would amuse the painter or make the musician better known'.

It is almost certainly because of that club, with its Proustian name, that the tycoon Bernard Arnault, an unwavering supporter of Berluti, became interested in the firm, to the point of buying it in 1993. He went on to make Olga Berluti an international star next to the acclaimed British houses John Lobb, Church's and Edward Green.

Alessandro Berluti

The Berluti story started in the late nineteenth century with the arrival in Paris of Alessandro Berluti, a young Italian bootmaker from the small village of Senigallia, on the Adriatic Coast. He did well in the booming *fin de siècle* atmosphere, and soon made the right acquaintances, creating shoes for fellow Italian bootmakers and the rich customers of the Paris luxury hotels.

In 1893 Berluti created a very out-of-the-ordinary model whose design surprised everyone:

a lace-up pump made from a single piece of leather without any visible stitching. It was named the Alessandro after its creator. This shoe remains an emblem of the house, and (next to John Lobb's double-buckle monk shoe, William) has certainly triggered many a gentleman's affair with shoes and sartorial passion. I must speak up on behalf of thousands of other Parisian gentlemen and make it known that it was most probably this shoe that inoculated me with the virus of elegance and provoked my craving for beautiful clothes.

Torello Berluti

Alessandro's son Torello was the initiator of this Franco-Italian shoe story in its official form. He started the business and set up shop – or rather *salon* – in rue du Mont Thabor, near the Jardin des Tuileries. He created a very bold Adelaide oxford in 1928, as well as a boot called Sans Gêne (meaning both 'shameless' and 'comfortable' in French), similar to the famous Churchill model made in London by George Cleverley, with elastic lateral vamps for a very snug fit.

Such daring models were an instant and resounding success. They were so popular that Torello's illustrious customers from the Plaza-Athénée or the Bristol hotels had to join a very long waiting list, and he even had to open a bigger *salon* to accommodate his expanding clientele, now made up of more and more famous people. He thus moved to 26 rue Marbeuf, a stone's throw from the Champs-Elysées and avenue Montaigne, and the publisher Gaston Gallimard, the playwright–painter Jean Cocteau and the Académie Française writer Marcel Achard made the trip there to buy their beloved shoes. Over the years others of the French crème de la crème would follow, and such film directors as François Truffaut, Jean-Luc Godard and Claude Chabrol thus became customers of Berluti's bespoke workshop.

Talbinio and Olga Berluti

After the Second World War Torello's son Talbinio, who had been trained in the art of bootmaking by his father, took the reins of the family business, launching the first line of ready-to-wear shoes in 1959. It was inspired by the house's bespoke production, and presented a refined and sophisticated approach to handmade men's shoes.

The collection was an instant success, and the concept of luxury ready-to-wear immediately appealed to a new set of customers whose hedonistic lifestyle was incompatible with the idea of waiting to fulfil their desires. Even the house's bespoke customers now had their eyes on these wonderfully appealing shoes, all the more so since they were instantly available.

It was in 1959 also that the young Olga Berluti, Talbinio's cousin, entered the family story. She did not seem destined to become an icon of bootmaking, but she soon made herself indispensable to the firm's stylish customers. As is customary in a traditional Italian family business, she started by performing menial tasks, in order to learn the ways of the trade. With her enthusiasm, frank nature and creative mind, not to mention her indomitable energy, it was not long before she had become the darling of fashionable Parisians.

In 1962 Olga created the famous Berluti loafer for Andy Warhol, the Andy. The artist had held his first solo exhibition at Eleanor Ward's Stable Gallery in New York that very year, a fact that showed Olga to have not just talent, but also taste and instinct. Warhol doted on his Berluti loafers, and he didn't fail to make that known to everyone under the sun.

During the 1970s and 1980s, in a series of spectacular moves, Olga introduced a string of innovations that established the dazzling Berluti style. Shoes were scarred or even tattooed, and the firm decided to use only one type of leather for its production: Venezia leather.

In-house colourists create custom patinas and colours.

The Andy loafer was created by Olga Berluti for Andy Warhol in 1962.

Berluti is no longer just a shoe brand or even a Parisian bootmaker. It has become a clothing style in its own right, creating a unique aesthetic experience with its own codes and rules – and it was Olga's genius that effected this transformation.

The Berluti Style

Berluti shoes are recognizable a mile away. Even if you don't know anything about shoes, they attract notice, especially that of women. Their unique character exerts extraordinary attraction and unheard-of sex appeal.

Berluti's vision is first and foremost grounded in sound shoemaking heritage. It is also based on a very imaginative stylistic vision that has shown exceptional consistency over the years. Among the firm's principles is a simple yet ground-breaking idea: 'Comfort is never compromised in the pursuit of elegance; the two principles are inextricably linked.' Aesthetics are nevertheless foremost at Berluti, and the firm never gives up on beauty in favour of sturdiness.

The embodiment of this principle is what many (myself included) regard as paramount in Berluti's permanent collection: the Alessandro shoe, the be-all and end-all of classic shoes. This whole-cut pump, made of a single piece of leather, was the first shoe to express the primary importance of shape and silhouette for men's shoes. Its upper – devoid of pieces, holes or stitching – presents a clean, clear visual sweep with no perceptible clash. The planed edge (where the sole follows the curved shape of the shoe, so that no extension peeps out along the sides) and the curving outline enhance the shape of the shoe last, which many consider to be the quintessence of high-end shoemaking.

As the firm's reputation grew, its pursuit of refinement and character involved extreme decisions, most notably the production of Blake-sewn shoes in its ready-to-wear lines. Blake construction, which is favoured by Italian shoemakers, involves stitching together the insole, upper and outsole, yielding finer shoes without extensions along the sides. There was much debate among shoe buffs about this construction, since it was known to be less durable than the Goodyear method used by British shoemakers.

The debate in fact concerned the difficulty of resoling a Blake shoe, as it is an arduous task to sew

This extraordinary leather was historically used mainly for luxury bookbinding, and requires special treatment and maintenance. Wearing it is a unique experience. Its main characteristic is its softness, which makes it an ideal material to absorb patina and allow colours to shimmer. It became Berluti's emblem, and Olga used it to create many variations, including such wonders as the calligraphy-inspired Scritto, which has become, quite literally, a signature model for the firm.

The house's various poetic collections over the years have reached fabulous levels of originality: the Empreinte du Loup (Wolf's Print), a series of soft, moccasin-style shoes inspired by Native American footwear; the Physiological shoes, designed for comfort without sacrificing style; and, more recently, the Esprit de la Couture, a virtuosic tribute to leather stitching in a decidedly Parisian style.

Since the turn of the twenty-first century Berluti has developed its range of small leather pieces. Its bags are particularly splendid (among them the quintessential briefcase called Deux Jours, of 2005), and use the Scritto technique to great effect.

A pair of Berluti ankle boots with a magnificent patina in many shades of brown.

the new sole using exactly the same holes. The welt in Goodyear construction, on the other hand, makes it easy. This points to a radical difference between British and Italian bootmakers: the former aim for comfort and durability; the latter focus on shape and elegance. (This difference of approach is obvious in tailoring, as well.)

Berluti's concept is of course at the vanguard of the Italian approach, and the firm has never wavered from its preference of aesthetics over sturdiness. That means that Berluti shoes can be delicate and should be worn in full consciousness, like any fine item. As a unique contribution to the world of men's shoes, this ought to be better appreciated. It is currently somewhat underrated, in striking contrast with the strong reputation of British shoes for comfort and sturdiness.

Olga Berluti boldly applied concepts taken from jewelry to men's shoes, thus giving a voice to a new generation of men for whom the elegance of footwear, whether flashy or sober, took precedence over its practicality. In that sense, the approach represented a minor aesthetic and sociological revolution – the sign that stylish men were back.

A Bespoke Workshop of International Rank

While Berluti was expanding internationally, it always kept its important bespoke bootmaking operation and recruited the masters in the field. Pierre Corthay (see page 118) was once among them, and Anthony Delos is a similar figure today.

In this glorious age of sartorial renaissance, the bespoke salon in rue Marbeuf is handsomely carrying the torch of French bootmaking, keeping it a superior and virtuosic trade and refining the Berluti style with every new shoe, presenting new models in the tradition of classic bootmaking but with a special, soulful touch. It is no wonder that a growing league of gentlemen hold the Berluti style in intense and faithful admiration.

Looking Ahead

Olga Berluti's contribution to contemporary men's style is huge, and not limited to luxury shoes. In 2011 she handed the reins of the Berluti world to the appropriately named Alessandro Sartori, whose mission it has been to develop the firm's stylistic heritage and apply it to men's clothing as a whole (see page 64).

This stylistic legacy is both deeply rooted in Italy and intensely Parisian. It has been so influential that everywhere in Paris, not just in rue Marbeuf or rue de Sèvres, the language has changed. . .and people now say *soulier*, not *chaussure*.

CORTHAY

The Hero of a Sartorial Revolution

For many lovers of refined footwear, Pierre Corthay is not simply a Parisian bootmaker with a worldwide reputation or the artistic director of a luxury house that bears his name. He is nothing less than a cultural hero. The very opposite of the commonplace contemporary entrepreneur driven by spreadsheets and business plans, he stands out as the archetypal artist and artisan, who believed in his destiny and made it happen through sheer force of purpose. In the case of Pierre Corthay, even that is rather an understatement.

As might be expected, Corthay's story is a handmade tale of great encounters. In 1990, with barely a penny in his pocket, he decided to buy the workshop of the Parisian bootmaker Henri Richomme, in rue Volney. He was then just beginning to make ends meet as head of the Berluti workshop, after six years of unpaid 'Tour de France' apprenticeship and eighteen months as a worker at John Lobb, and didn't have the wherewithal to acquire the workshop of Monsieur Richomme, who wanted to find someone young to take over on his retirement. That sort of practical detail was not going to stop Corthay, however, and he worked out an old-school deal with the ageing bootmaker, who agreed to be paid in instalments. Corthay thus bought the workshop, paying each instalment as the customers slowly trickled in, earning his independence shoe by shoe.

Suzy Menkes, Pierre Corthay's Lucky Star

For Corthay, the first two years were tough. He had yet to make a name for himself, and the market for bespoke shoes was far from thriving. Customers who knew about such a refined product were few and far between, even near place Vendôme. According to Corthay, he made only 'one and a half pairs of shoes per month', hardly enough to pay his instalments and expenses. It was impossible to pay himself a salary, let alone employ anyone else.

And yet Corthay's life took a radical turn thanks to Stéphane, the paradoxically famous owner of a little underground second-hand clothing boutique in the Batignolles area of Paris, a word-of-mouth address among connoisseurs for thirty years. In this rare place one can find wonderful vintage treats, such as bespoke Savile Row suits or clothes from the best Parisian houses, including Cifonelli, Camps de Luca, Smalto and Charvet.

One day in 1992 none other than the great Suzy Menkes, then fashion editor for the *International*

Corthay's two-eyelet derby Arca is the signature shoe of the house and one of its best sellers of all time. This black version has red piping and laces.

Herald Tribune, pushed that secret yet illustrious door in search of a Parisian bootmaker for an article she was writing. Stéphane told her that she absolutely must go and see a young bootmaker who had just set up shop and who promised great things: Pierre Corthay.

The conversation changed Corthay's destiny. Not only did the high priestess of fashion fall in love with Corthay's work, but also she let the whole world know about it. A few days later her article appeared on the back cover of the *International Herald Tribune*. In the little workshop on rue Volney the hitherto mute telephone started to ring, and it never stopped. A few months later the sultan of Brunei ordered 150 pairs of bespoke shoes, and Lanvin farmed its bespoke orders out to Corthay. The world had just discovered his incredible genius.

Ups and Downs

Thirteen years after Corthay's unconventional acquisition of Richomme's workshop, in 2003, history repeated itself. He was not happy with the Italian subcontractor in charge of his ready-to-wear collection, which had just been launched and was

getting some attention. He therefore decided, rather impulsively, to open his own factory near Paris so as to be able to control the whole process. Yet again, he was far from having the financial capacity for such a venture. And yet again, it was his craft that provided the solution, with a little help from his brother Christophe, who is also a Compagnon du Devoir, and 'Toulousain', another bootmaking Compagnon, who was there from the start. They managed to put together the funds they needed thanks to a providential order from the American tycoon Robert Rubin.

Rubin had just opened his famous private golf club, the Bridge, in the Hamptons in New York State, and wanted to offer the first sixty members a pair of bespoke golf shoes to make up for the planned lack of golf carts (after all, the membership cost each person about $750,000 – before tax). Rubin, who was a great admirer of Corthay's, paid for the full order in advance. Thus, without the support of any bank or investors, but thanks to this one order – and the toil and sweat entailed in handmaking those sixty pairs of golf shoes in just a few months – Corthay managed to acquire his own factory in Neuilly-Plaisance, just outside Paris.

Pierre Corthay, photographed by Andy Barnham.

At Corthay's factory in Beaupréau in central France, twenty-seven artisans, last-makers, designers, pattern-cutters, clickers, closers and cobblers produce bench-made Goodyear shoes that are among the most refined in the world.

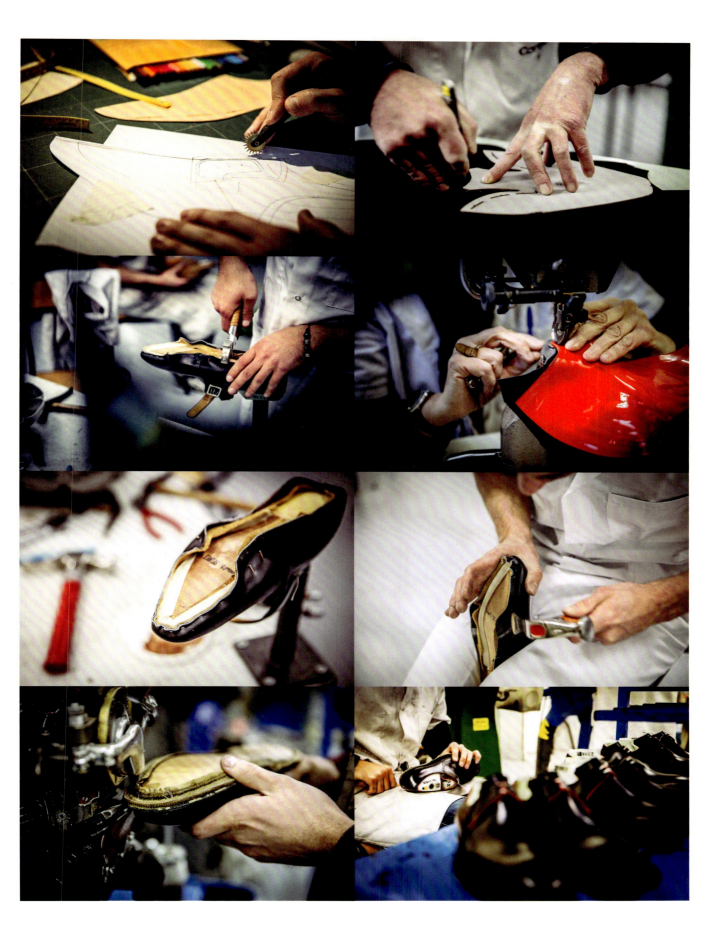

Corthay's story sounds like a fairy tale, full of magic encounters, inspired business decisions, lean spells, hard work and happenstance. In 2008 and 2009, however, the fairy tale turned to a nightmare when the Japanese market dropped dramatically and its orders suddenly stopped, putting the firm in jeopardy and forcing the factory to slow down its operations. Corthay's maverick life course and off-the-wall career took another turn – one that probably made more economic sense – when, in October 2010, Xavier de Royère, a discreet but active businessman, stepped in. He was then an executive of Loewe, the Spanish leather goods company, and bought Corthay's company, bailing it out and taking it to even greater international fame.

For the Love of Leather

As young as eight years of age, Corthay had become enamoured with leather, and spent his Wednesdays having tea with one of his father's cousins, who owned a small leather goods workshop. At that time Brussels rules and regulations did not reign supreme in workshops, and so the boy was able to touch and use real tools under the supervision of his cousin. At thirteen, yearning for independence and full of entrepreneurial spirit, he built a small workshop in his own bedroom and started making small leather pieces – belts, purses and card-holders – which he sold (or gave away to girls he fancied!).

It was only logical that Corthay should join the Confrérie des Compagnons du Devoir and start his own apprenticeship as a bootmaker, a craft he

deems to be 'the most comprehensive' of all the distinguished skills that are taught and passed on by this unique corporation of artisans. 'At the time', he says, 'I was the odd one out in the corporation. In the late 1970s the skilled manual trades were not well regarded among the French youth. In the school system, opting for that sort of trade was seen as a failure and not a means to learning a noble craft. It is as true now as it was then – for reasons of standing, the parents would rather have their children study law or business.'

Corthay's Masters

Six years of apprenticeship and travelling took Corthay all over France: the Old Port of Marseille for two years, then Toulouse in the south-west, La Roche-Bernard in Brittany, Lyon, Strasbourg and, lastly, Paris. Like all those who complete their Tour de France apprenticeship, he has fond memories of those intense times, as well as an enduring respect for the masters who welcomed him and taught him the techniques of the trade.

Jean Dréan

The old bootmaking master Jean Dréan is a very special member of Corthay's personal pantheon. He lived in the small town of La Roche-Bernard in Morbihan, and was the last member of a family spanning nine generations of bootmakers, who had plied their trade continuously since 1705. An awe-inspiring character if ever there was one, as Corthay explains:

A pair of purple Arcas is ready to be delivered.

I had heard about him thanks to one of my companion brothers and I had my mind set on working with him before he was too old. I wrote again and again asking for work and after being rebuffed many times, as he considered himself too old for it, I finally talked him into having me in his workshop for a summer, without wages, just accommodation.

For three summers I lived with him, ate with him and worked with him to perfect my technique and sharpen the precision of each gesture. Jean Dréan was the one who really taught me the basics of this craft. Working with him was like a final internship. It was only after that that I felt ready to take the big leap and start out professionally.

In 1984, with his toolbox under his arm, Corthay knocked on the door of John Lobb's Paris workshop, where he met the great Georges William Dickinson, then the general director of the most respected bootmaking institution in Paris. It was a difficult period for the shoe trade: the older generation of workers was nearing retirement, and fewer and fewer people were choosing the craft. The workshop employed a number of accomplished veteran bootmakers who worked at home. In these circumstances, Dickinson did not hesitate to give the young man a chance to shine. Corthay started as an apprentice stitcher under the tutelage of 'Monsieur Louis' Portella, a great workshop manager of the time.

Corthay remembers his brief year-and-a-half stint at Lobb's with great affection, especially the various colourful characters whose names he can still recall thirty years later: David, Gaspard, Laurent, 'Monsieur Yves', 'Madame Marie-Claude':

When the old bootmakers were coming to the workshop for their delivery, the young apprentices that we were leapt on their shoes to scrutinize each and every detail and learn as much as possible from their work. Can you imagine that these artisans had been trained before the war? Their skills were like an endangered species. I was ever so lucky to have known such magnificent craftsmen before they disappeared.

Jean Bourles

In 1985, barely a year and a half after arriving at John Lobb's, Corthay received a phone call from Dréan's former closer, who was then working for Berluti. Since he was retiring, he suggested

Left to right: Three Corthay bespoke shoes, the Belphegor 'Ghillie-like' shoe, a single-buckle monk strap and a full brogue oxford with silk laces and an eagle-claw last; the wingtip of the ready-to-wear Vendôme brogue is positioned very far to the front of the shoe.

that Corthay join the Berluti workshop and work under Jean Bourles. This major figure in the trade had trained with the legendary Roger Vivier, the footwear genius who invented stilettoes, created the pattern for Dior pumps and made the titillating thigh-high boots sported by Brigitte Bardot for the song 'Harley Davidson' in the 1960s.

Famous for his meticulous approach, Bourles turned out to be Corthay's second major influence, passing on his taste for excellence and exacting perfection. A year later, in 1986, Pierre stepped into the great Bourles's shoes as manager of the bespoke workshop. He stayed there for six years, until one of the firm's suppliers, the last-maker Max Hameline, told him that the old bootmaker Richomme wanted to retire and was looking for someone to replace him.

The Corthay Style

Having honed his craft at John Lobb and then Berluti, Pierre Corthay soon forged a unique style that merged these antithetical visions of men's footwear. While Berluti was adroitly and brazenly developing a flamboyant yet graceful approach with unusual patinas and radical shapes, John Lobb flew the flag for traditional bootmaking, leading the educated Parisian troops of classic style. Corthay simply took the best of both worlds, creating shapes and patterns that displayed a very strong personality.

The Sergio derby was conceived in 1996 for a famous photographers' agent, and represents the typical Corthay style. It is at first sight a classic shoe. But its elegant, gently sloping toe bridges the gap between the 'eagle claw' toe (created by the near-mythical Hungarian bootmaker in London, Nikolaus Tuczek, in the 1930s) and the conservative British toe.

The Vendôme oxford displays a wingtip at the furthest fore of the foot so as to give a streamlined shape. It is among the house's classic models, as is the Belphegor, a well-known pattern that echoes the Scottish ghillie (the traditional shoe to wear with a kilt). This model with its special lacing is striking, especially the sophisticated Satan version with its 'pinched' tip, for which the bootmaker must heat the leather and pinch it during the few seconds when it is hot enough. Talk about technical brinkmanship!

Icon

In 1999 Corthay made a bespoke model that remains to this day his greatest success: the Arca. Then, in 2003, he released a ready-to-wear version of

Overleaf

An orange patent-leather Arca is pictured with the Eiffel Tower in the background. Corthay is the rising star of Parisian high-end shoes.

The entrepreneur extraordinaire Xavier de Royère gave Corthay a second wind in 2010.

Spectacular bicoloured, bi-leather Corthay Vendôme shoes.

this two-eyelet derby with its elegantly pure lines, beautifully designed tongue and remarkably delicate Goodyear welting. It marked the beginning of Corthay's international recognition. The Arca, which now comes in many versions, has become a classic of men's luxury footwear, the emblem of men's new-found love for beautiful shoes.

Looking Forward

At the end of 2010, when Xavier de Royère became the controlling shareholder of Maison Corthay, he gave the firm the possibility of truly international expansion. He and his team opened several boutiques in major cities, including London, Hong Kong, Dubai and Beijing, and defined a business structure that enabled long-term strategy. Corthay was thus able to focus on design and artistic direction, while the bespoke workshop is still run by his faithful companions, his brother Christophe and Toulousain as workshop manager. In 2013 the firm's factory, where traditional Goodyear welting still reigns supreme, moved to Beaupréau in Maine-et-Loire, western France.

In just a few years Maison Corthay has achieved unprecedented international expansion and has reached the status of benchmark for footwear connoisseurs all over the world.

Maître d'Art

In 2008 the French ministry of Culture and Communication made Corthay Maître d'Art (Master Craftsman). This distinction, which has been awarded to 100 individual artisans (and not to their companies), singles out exceptional craftsmen in France and draws its inspiration from the Japanese living national treasures (*Kakko Nintei*). Corthay's craftsmanship has thus been recognized as an essential part of France's heritage.

But the treasure he protects and carries within him is nothing other than the savoir-faire of nine generations of Dréans bootmakers, of Bourles's demanding precision, of John Lobb's old pre-war workers' bootmaking secrets, and of the wisdom of all the masters Corthay encountered during his apprenticeship. Corthay likes to quote an old African saying: 'When an old man dies, a library burns.' Thanks to his decisions, interests and activities, the 'libraries' of Dréan, Bourles and countless others have escaped the flames of oblivion.

AUBERCY

Family Business

Rue Vivienne is a pleasant street in the very heart of Paris, five minutes' walk from the Palais Brongniart (the former stock exchange), and not far from the place du Palais Royal. At number 34, a fine old wooden shopfront with two display windows features a dazzlingly elegant array of men's shoes.

In one window, sitting next to a beautiful pair of two-tone buttoned Balmoral boots, a diminutive sign with gold lettering on a small piece of black leather presents a statement from another era: 'The best advertising is a satisfied customer.' The first time I read that note, I couldn't help but think of the ads of yesteryear, of my childhood, which were all about reputation and renown. I smiled and wondered if the presence of that little card, printed in small letters and sitting on a minute stand, had not been simply forgotten since the 1950s.

That was my first visit to Aubercy at 34 rue Vivienne. And even though I knew about the quality of its shoes thanks to my online magazine, *Parisian Gentleman*, I had never set foot there and didn't yet understand why that address was so close to the hearts of classic shoe lovers.

Founded in 1935 by Renée and André Aubercy, this boutique devoted to luxury shoes has occupied the same address since the very beginning, and has a worldwide reputation that could not be imagined from the size of the premises. The shop has been handed down from father to son: André, Philippe and now Xavier Aubercy. This small *maison* stands out as a very special place in the world of luxury men's shoes, even though its yearly output is limited to a few hundred pairs.

The small note in the window, reminiscent of Magritte in its 'This is not an ad' spirit, sets the tone. This is a place for connoisseurs, for people with a passion. Welcome to the Aubercys'.

The Bagatelle Centre

André Aubercy's initial calling had nothing to do with luxury shoes, but he rubbed shoulders very early in his professional life with an elite clientele whose demanding taste would make his name in the shoe business later on. In the 1920s, after serving in the Bataillon de Joinville (a French military unit for top-level sportsmen), he decided to open a fitness centre for Parisian high society. To attract the affluent and selective clientele he wanted, he opened his health club on the top floor of an elegant building in the Bagatelle neighbourhood. Choosing a stately upper-class building for a gym was daring,

An impromptu guest (a Parisian pigeon) visits the beautiful Aubercy boutique on rue Vivienne.

but it was probably the key to getting the attention of such distinguished gentlemen as the Duke of Windsor and Albert Sarraut, an important politician during the Third Republic.

Throughout the 1920s Aubercy offered fitness training to Paris's crème de la crème: the most influential aristocrats, politicians and businessmen as well as the pick of the wealthy and idle dandies of the time. This may have been a sporting environment, but the sophistication of Aubercy's clients implied that he associated with numerous important figures. One encounter was a decisive one, with a rich collector and patron of the arts who became his friend for life: the full-time dandy Arturo Lopez.

Renée and André Aubercy Open a Boutique

In 1935, while her husband was training the Parisian beau monde in his gym, Renée Aubercy opened a men's shoe shop at 34 rue Vivienne, with a friend of the family who would become their son Philippe's godmother. Thus it was Renée who created the family business, first stepping into the world of luxury shoes that was to become the family's obsession.

In 1937 and 1938 the political climate quickly took a turn for the worse, and affluent Jews began leaving the country in a hurry. André Aubercy decided to close his gym and work with his wife at the shop. By dint of hard work and perseverance, the couple struggled through the war and the ensuing hardship of food rationing and deprivation

'The best advertising is a satisfied customer', says the small sign in the window of Aubercy's shop.

Aubercy has gained a
worldwide reputation for
the quality and originality
of its shoes.

of all sorts, managing to build a solid clientele
of businessmen from the nearby stock exchange.
Aubercy's reputation for reliability and high quality
started growing among those involved in business
and financial affairs.

The Aubercys produced their shoes in Santos, a
small factory near the Parc de Buttes-Chaumont in
Paris. That small family workshop was where André
met the man who would teach him everything:
Gilbert Maginot, a pattern-cutter and closer.
Maginot (whose great-uncle gave his name to the
French army's unfortunate line of defence during
the Second World War) became a friend of André's
and took the time to teach him the challenging
technical side of the shoe business. This friendship
even resulted in André's son Philippe meeting
Odette, who worked with Maginot and who later

became Madame Aubercy, an iconic figure
of the Aubercy business.

Lopez's Present

In post-war Parisian circles Arturo Lopez was
already a legend. The heir of a Chilean industrial
family, this prince of Parisian socialites was a great
collector of art and furniture as well as a generous
patron of the arts. He is well known for having
donated often and generously to the Palace of
Versailles.

The man who was notoriously but unofficially
Lopez's companion, Alexis de Rédé, was known
for his elegance and extravagant passion for the
London bootmaker Nikolaus Tuczek and his disciple
George Cleverley, and owned a large collection of
their shoes. In fact, Baron de Rédé, who was also

AUBERCY

Aubercy's main boutique is on rue Vivienne in Paris.

Since most Aubercy shoes are made to order, all combinations of pattern, leather and construction are possible, as these examples on the shop's round table show.

famous for his delicate feet and the sheer elegance of his shoes, made Cleverley's name in France. Everybody in his circle wanted to have shoes as refined as the baron's.

Lopez, meanwhile, himself the owner of an impressive collection of shoes bought from the same London masters, made the kind gesture of offering several pairs to his friend André Aubercy so that he could draw inspiration from the very best shoes of the time. These private collections were the source of the magnificent examples of bootmaking that still sit like powerful talismans in the boutique on rue Vivienne and in Philippe Aubercy's study. The firm's unique shoes are also a tribute to Lopez, who – however indirectly – greatly influenced its style, and whose character rests in the refinement, even delicacy of its models.

L'Avventura Italiana

In 1956 André Aubercy, who was known for his strenuous efforts to provide his customers with the best products he could find (sometimes even at his own cost), decided to try out the renowned skill of Italian shoemakers when he sought a new workshop for his shoes. His decision was motivated by the closure of the Santos workshop in Paris and also by the desire to take a step up in quality and to bring renewed creativity and flair to his firm's shoes.

True to his way of doing things, and contrary to that of many of his colleagues, he did not just pick models in an Italian workshop. He took pains

to select a partner with whom he could work, a workshop where he could apply his own methods, develop his own shapes and patterns and eventually give shape to his own artistic vision.

It was at that time that Aubercy was truly making a name for itself, asserting its own style. André was becoming his own man, and his new Italian workshop allowed him to offer his customers complete freedom of choice in model, shape, hide and pattern.

In 1961 Aubercy sent Philippe to Italy for a year, and then for another year to England, to hone his skill in the two leading countries for men's shoes. In 1970 Philippe took over the firm with his wife, Odette, and carried on in the same spirit, offering his clients a wide choice while maintaining the highest standards.

The Aubercy Style

The Aubercy style is typically Parisian, at the crossroads of the British and Italian approaches. The British school, superbly epitomized by Tuczek, Cleverley, Lobb and others, has always focused on the triple doctrine of 'restrained, comfortable, durable' shoes, while the Italian school has always been obsessed with style and refinement. Somewhere between the forthright rigour of the British, sometimes lacking in polish and seduction, and the polished seduction of the Italians, sometimes lacking in forthrightness and rigour, Aubercy has struck a balance. Its brogues are not as sturdy and severe as

Crazy Lace by Aubercy.

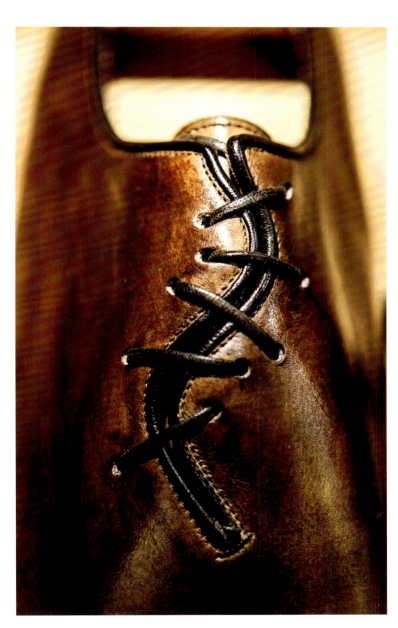

those by the British, but they are still recognizably brogues, while their loafers are obviously less slender than the Italians' but remain marvellously graceful and well-proportioned.

The Aubercys – fathers and sons – have not been content with just that balancing act, however. They have managed to create an original approach that represents more than the reconciliation of the British and Italian styles. They have reached the quintessential Parisian style, at once sober and sophisticated.

The Swan, one of their most famous models, is a perfect example of their originality. It's a five-eyelet oxford with a straight toecap, devoid of brogueing, built on a very classic last, whose sober pattern stands out as a model of restrained elegance. Despite this apparent sobriety, it uses top-band stitching, which means stitching the inside of the upper so that the stitches are not visible at all, finishing off the shoe with a very neat line. It's a typically Parisian shoe: severe at first sight, wonderfully sophisticated at second glance.

The James is for me one of the most beautiful oxfords on the market today, displaying the same character of apparent sobriety with built-in sophistication. This amazingly classic model is assembled using a 'lollipop' last, a shape typically favoured by London bootmakers, with a low-key pattern that stretches on a large surface of leather, making the shoe very slender and formal. This model, so Parisian in its balanced refinement, features a hand-sewn welt (impressively, a Goodyear stitch without using machine stitching at all).

Because of its small size, and the impressive technical quality of its Italian workshop, Aubercy can provide all types of construction. It offers Blake,

Goodyear, Norwegian, hand-sewn welt and even a mixture of Blake and Goodyear, a rare feat on the shoe market.

Family Business

The day I first visited the Aubercy boutique, I was lucky enough to be welcomed by the whole family: Philippe, Odette and their son Xavier, who took over in 1995. Xavier is a warm and endearing character, the rare kind who shares his feelings, opinions and passion with disarming candour and complete openness. After taking over the management, he decided to take the company even higher, and in 2014 he restarted the bespoke line, with the Japanese bootmaker Yasuhiro Shiota working in the boutique itself.

Xavier is responsible for bringing into the catalogue designs of a more and more daring spirit. He has a particular penchant for unorthodox patterns, such as the arresting Besteguy, a spectacular half-derby, and the Crazy Lace, a whole-cut oxford with asymmetrical lacing.

On that September morning, the three hours I spent visiting the shop, including two hours in Philippe's study, listening to him talk eloquently and lyrically about his love of men's luxury shoes, showed me what Aubercy is about. I was electrified, astonished, bedazzled – and heart-struck, too.

I do not know whether Aubercy will one day become a company with a global dimension, and whether the family can ever accept anonymous investors as part of their family business to develop this beautiful and still slightly underground brand so that it reaches the mainstream. What I do know, however, is that at 34 rue Vivienne a local family is offering some of the most beautiful shoes in the world. 'The best advertising is a satisfied customer', says the note in the window. After spending some time at Aubercy's, I think I understand.

Philippe Aubercy, his wife, Odette, and their son Xavier.

The in-house bespoke bootmaker works on a last.

Aubercy's in-house Japanese bespoke master bootmaker, Yasuhiro Shiota.

J. M. WESTON

A National Treasure

Weston is a wealthy suburb of Boston, Massachusetts, with a little above 11,000 souls. The small town is locally famous for having the highest per capita income in the whole state, for its very low crime rate and for the excellence of its schools. Although this affluent area promotes its colleges and quality of life, it is likely that very few of its inhabitants know that their town is actually much more famous 6,000 kilometres (3,700 miles) away, in France, more precisely in the lovely little city of Limoges in the west-centre of the country.

In France, Weston is considered essential, its name synonymous with excellence, consistency and craftsmanship. The brand has come to represent the epitome of high-quality footwear even for the original connoisseurs, by which I mean that handful of brands present during the 1980s, when the market for luxury men's shoes was in its very early stages and had not yet taken off.

At that time, there was a ubiquitous advertisement for cheap shoes that claimed 'You'd have to be mad to spend more', a true hymn to mass consumption. In that context, J. M. Weston could not be a high-street name, but rather a brand about which only a select few — the genuine shoe experts — knew.

As a stalwart Weston man, I have vivid memories of that time, especially when I think of my fellow students' looks of dismay when I told them that I was saving penny after penny to be able to buy myself a pair of Weston shoes, the Chasse (Hunting) model, which I considered one of the most beautiful in the history of footwear.

I can also remember the price: 5,000 French francs, an amount my friends found surreal, since none of them had ever spent more than 100 francs on a pair of shoes. They found it very weird that I should be ranting and raving about Norwegian stitch, waxed linen thread, butted apron and vegetable tanning.

Thirty-five years on, the Weston Chasse, with its round line, gorgeous pattern and still indestructible stitching, remains a reference point for many specialists in classic elegance. And the celebrated 180 loafer — the most highly acclaimed European penny loafer — is still worn by a great number of executives in Paris's business districts. J. M. Weston is among the true legends of fine French footwear.

This contemporary Adelaide oxford by J. M. Weston displays a sophisticated pattern on a modern last and is designed by the firm's in-house artistic director, Michel Perry.

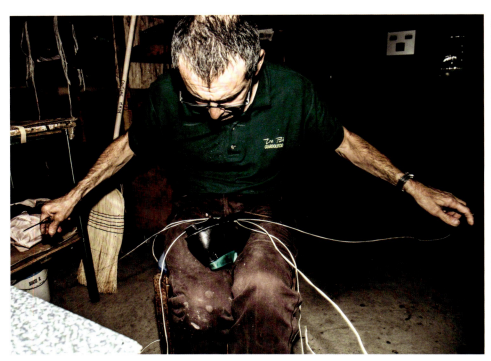

The Blanchard Family and Jean Viard: How J. M. Weston Was Born

It was one Edouard Blanchard, a bootmaker by trade, who created the company in 1891 in Limoges, where he opened a shoe factory. Corporate legend has it that it was his son Eugène who gave the company its name, after a three-year stay in the Massachusetts town in 1904. There he learned the technique of Goodyear welting before coming back to France to take over as head of the family factory.

After his father's death, Eugène decided to reduce the firm's shoe production from 600 to 80 pairs a day, so that shoes by J. M. Weston, a name he patented in 1922, could be immediately recognized for the superiority of their construction.

At about the same time, Blanchard met Jean Viard, an eminent dandy in Paris's high society, who would become a great name in French footwear. Their association turned out to be essential to the development and success of Weston. The two men became business partners and opened their first shop on boulevard de Courcelles. Later, in 1932, they opened another on the most beautiful avenue in the world, at 114 avenue des Champs-Elysées.

The house style was radically British, as this represented the height of elegance in the mind of the French clientele. That time was indeed the acme of London bootmakers, such as the feted (and yet somewhat obscure) Nikolaus Tuczec on Clifford Street, for thirty-eight years the boss of a certain George Cleverley, and who made his name producing delicate brogues with chiselled toes.

The classic Weston models bear names that clearly recall this British inspiration, at a time when aristocrats and high society wore outfits and shoes appropriate to their pastimes: a 'hunting' model for hunting, 'half-hunting' for outdoors and 'golf' shoes for that sport so favoured among the elite.

The Janson de Sailly: The First French Penny Loafer

It was during the 1960s, however, that J. M. Weston gave birth to the most celebrated of its models, the 180 loafer. During the 1950s, penny loafers had spread over American university campuses, especially in the Ivy League. The exact origin of the name is lost in the mist of history, although a believable urban legend suggests that students liked to insert a penny inside the diamond-shaped slit on

A Weston shoemaker works on a hand-welted pair of shoes. Some emblematic models of the house, including the Chasse derby, are strictly made by hand.

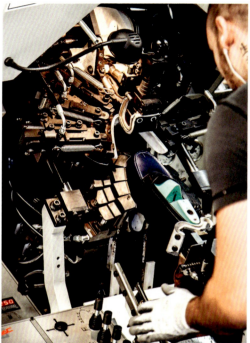

Artisans work at Weston's model factory in Limoges.

The process of making model 180, J. M. Weston's emblematic penny loafer.

Overleaf

J. M. Weston's beautiful archive collection of shoes is photographed in Limoges in 2014.

the saddle of the shoe so they would always have money to use in a telephone booth. The English company Wildsmith explains that this type of slip-on shoe is actually derived from a casual house shoe designed for King George VI in 1926; but so many bootmakers claim the invention that it is impossible to assert without a shadow of a doubt which company first created it.

What is undeniable is the way Weston, with brio and flair, made popular the Janson de Sailly loafer in the 1960s and continued to enjoy success with it since then. Janson de Sailly is the name of an upper-class school on rue de la Pompe in Paris's exclusive 16th arrondissement, whose pupils, most of them from affluent backgrounds, endorsed the 180 loafer. In much the same way, they embraced Shetland jumpers from Arnys, tight-fitting jackets from Renoma and Mini Cooper cars – in short, a French version of the American preppy style.

But while most of the defining features and accessories of the 1960s young trendies were gradually relegated to the pages of the inevitably transient and fleeting history of student fashion, Weston's 180 loafer did not disappear. Better yet, it survived all trends and fads, inspiring generation

after generation (and even appealing to all generations simultaneously). It is a cultural icon; and it is also the only ready-to-wear penny loafer in the world to come in seven different widths.

What Makes Weston Unique

Weston is not just any footwear company, and it stands out clearly, and in many ways, from its British, Spanish and Italian competitors. It is the only company in the world with its own tanning factory, where it produces soles of legendary sturdiness. (The Bastin tanning factory is actually the last to use vegetable tanning in Europe.) Weston is the only brand to offer different widths – usually five – for each half-size. It is also famous for being the official supplier of the French Republican Guard and the police's motorcycle division, the best-loved security forces in the country.

As for the firm's superb factory, it has always – through thick and thin – been in Limoges. It is one of the most beautiful in the world and certainly one of the rare places that can compete with the best factories of Northamptonshire. In it, shoes are produced the way they should be, the way my late grandfather loved to see them made – and I hope

An exotic-skin oxford.

Premium hides wait for the clicker, the artisan in charge of cutting the shape of the shoe's upper.

The Limoges factory also undertakes the difficult art of equestrian bootmaking. J. M. Weston is the official boot supplier to the famous French Republican Guard, an elite group of military horseriders dedicated to supporting the most important state ceremonies in Paris.

he still enjoys the spectacle from the next world. Machines are used to help artisans in their most taxing tasks. The rest of the 150 different processes by which a shoe is made up follow the strict standards of traditional bootmaking.

As for my favourite model, the Chasse, which I eventually purchased (much later than expected), it is still made entirely by hand by the few craftsmen who are able to master the demanding technique of Norwegian welting.

The Weston Style

A staunch advocate of the British style until the late 1980s, Weston gradually moved towards a more 'continental' style in the mid-1990s, and eventually came out as a fully Parisian house when Michel Perry became artistic director in 2001. While the

eternal classics have been maintained as part of the house style and still contribute to Weston's reputation and success, Perry's bold creations have added an unmistakably Parisian flair. His Graphic line contains superbly modern oxfords with a high upper, while the Conti line is even bolder in shape, stitching and pattern; his influence can also be seen in collections with a distinctly casual approach.

Jean-Louis Descours (1916–2013), who was at the helm of Weston for many years, used to say that 'five pairs can be enough for a lifetime'. My passion for fine footwear prevented me from ever being satisfied with just five pairs, but of course the Westons I bought in the late 1990s are still in perfect shape, and they will probably still be around long after I'm not. Weston is nothing less than a national treasure.

DIMITRI GOMEZ

Hidden Parisian Gem

Dimitri Gomez is among those very rare Parisian bootmakers whose reputation has long been established abroad. Despite this, his business is still carried out from a tiny workshop on rue Pasquier, part of the Parisian boutique of the famous British shoemaker Crockett & Jones.

Anyone who has had the chance or insight to push the door of his miniscule workshop can testify to the impressive quality of his shoes, as well as to the resonant, slightly rasping voice and wry humour of the man himself. As it happens, his shop is next door to the street's other unmissable character: Marc Guyot. The two are often to be found having lunch together in a wine bar near the Madeleine, discussing the length of a good Bourgogne, the pattern of a v-front derby or the merits of an exotic hide.

Gomez may explain that he came to work in the field of bespoke shoes purely by chance. However, it is obvious that he is at heart a true artisan and artist, with a passion for his work fuelled by a radical approach.

It All Started in London

A disappointment in love drove the young Gomez, then twenty-five, to move to London to put himself back together. There, he discovered traditional workshops, especially John Lobb's, where (contrary to received ideas) many young women work. Gomez was already attracted by footwear, and even boasted a remarkable collection of high-quality shoes. This trip would change his life altogether, making him ready to embrace the career of bootmaker. On leaving London he joined an orthopaedics school in Romans, France, where he worked with full wages, becoming a last-maker and prosthesis-maker.

Learning from the Elders

Gomez is one of a generation of bootmakers (with Pierre Corthay and Philippe Atienza) who had the luck to learn their craft from distinguished elders of the trade, the workers at Lobb's, Turks and Italians from Paris who had trained before the Second World War and remained the keepers of crafts that have all but disappeared today. Only a few staunch radicals, among them Gomez, still keep those methods alive.

As young as he was, Gomez already had a strong character and knew he was not interested in the prosthesis side of his job in Romans. What he liked was the stitching and the pattern-making,

Crocodile-skin bespoke shoe with tassels and two ghillie-type eyelets.

An exotic skin
v-front derby.

Dimitri Gomez, seen
here at work in his small
workshop in Paris, is a
rare artisan who crafts
his shoes exclusively by
hand and according to the
traditional techniques of
bespoke bootmaking.

everything that makes an elegant man's shoe, not
medical shoes. He thus opted for bootmaking, and
so in 1988, for his first internship, joined the ranks of
a renowned Parisian company that no longer exists:
Di Mauro.

The Sicilian bootmaker Camillo Di Mauro had
opened his business at 14 rue du Faubourg Saint-
Honoré in 1939. He was the darling shoemaker
of show business (having catered to such cinema
and theatre stars as the actor Sacha Guitry)
and, according to the media – which has always
been prone to hyperbole – nothing less than the
'Michelangelo of Shoes'.

Di Mauro plied his trade with his daughter
Tannina and two other workers. He was a true artist,
but also a passionate man. His shop was more
bootmaking curiosity cabinet than workshop, and
displayed such strange items as a musical shoe and
a mini-shoe (2 cm/less than 1 in. long, and weighing
less than a gram). That workshop is gone now, sadly,
but one can imagine the kind of environment where
Gomez learned the tools of his trade and gained his
reputation as a bespoke bootmaker. As was the rule,
as an apprentice he started out cleaning shoes,
performing simple repairs and maintenance operations
and cutting out a few mid-soles. But Gomez had
one precious advantage: he is a fast learner and has

always been keen to improve his skill. At night, after
the shop closed, he was still at work, with the help of
the older bootmakers, learning to stitch toecaps and
quarters, making real shoes and taking classes with
the Compagnons du Devoir.

Capo Bianco and the Paris Opera

In the mid-1990s another shoemaker, Capo Bianco,
renowned for its work with the Paris Opéra, would
give special orders to Di Mauro, especially those
for the star dancers' character shoes. These shoes

are worn on stage by dancers when they are not using ballet slippers, and when they practise 'character dancing', a form of dance inspired by folk traditions and enriched by the techniques of classical ballet. These shoes, which are made in aniline lambskin, by nature demand great precision in their construction, as they must fit the dancer's foot perfectly. Gomez was taught this very specific craft at Di Mauro's.

In the mid-1990s, however, Di Mauro was about to close as there were no heirs in the family and no buyers to keep the company going. The Opéra needed to find a solution. With a little help from the famous shoe-repair specialist Vaneau, Gomez helped to transfer this very special business to small premises near the Opéra, and carried on

making character shoes for the greatest names in the world of dancing, both Parisian and international, such as Marie-Claude Pietragalla and Patrick Dupond.

From Crockett & Jones to Dimitri Bottier

The turning point in Gomez's destiny came in 1998, when the late Thierry Duhesme asked him to join the Crockett & Jones boutique and open a salon of traditional bootmaking inside the Northampton company's main shop. Since then Gomez has stayed in the rue Pasquier. In his tiny workshop he produces entirely handmade shoes that stand among the most perfect and most sophisticated in the world. He is an exceptional artisan for connoisseurs.

THE
ART
OF
TRAVEL

4

Page 156

A late nineteenth-
century Moynat trunk.

An early twentieth-
century Moynat
advertisement offers
'everything for
the journey'.

The house's iconic
historical trunks
are displayed in the
Parisian *maison de
vente* (saleroom).

Trunks are intriguing and mysterious objects.
Anyone who has ever been fortunate enough to
touch, use and admire a late nineteenth-century
trunk must have felt that special something that is
more than the appreciation of a fine piece of luggage.

It is as if the travels the trunk has made during its
life are impressed into the fibre of its wood, leather,
canvas or metal.

From ancient times until the early nineteenth
century, trunks were used when making long trips.
Because they were custom-made, they enabled
travellers to carry everything they wanted: clothes,
hats, jewels, beauty products, shoes, musical
instruments, alcohol, silverware, money (there were
even trunk safes) and any other useful or valuable
thing dear to the travellers-cum-adventurers or
crowned heads of the time.

Trunks were at first heavy things, cumbersome
and unwieldy, that were not meant to be carried by
a single person and were handled only by servants.
As modes of transportation changed, so did luggage,
becoming lighter and more practical. Train and
aeroplane racks and ship's cabins were becoming
smaller, a fact that challenged luggage-makers to
come up with lightweight and ingenious pieces,
more portable and less bulky.

At the beginning of the twentieth century
luggage was still handled by porters or servants. It
was not until the true democratization of transport
(especially the law that established paid holiday
in France in 1936) that a trunk became a piece of
luggage that could be carried by a single person.

French Trunks:
The International Standard

French trunk-makers, particularly those of Paris,
have a very special place in the history of luggage.
In the mid-nineteenth century hundreds of baggage-
makers sprang up in the United States, England
and many European countries in response to the
radical transformation of transport. Despite that,
though, no great company has ever arisen in any
of those regions to compare with the historic
Parisian makers: Goyard, Louis Vuitton and, more
recently, Moynat (an old Parisian company that
was given a new lease of life by the Arnault group
in the early 2010s).

Most of the great American companies –
Belber, Seward Trunk Co., Rhino Trunk & Case,
Goldsmith & Son and Oshkosh Trunks, to name but
a few – died out during the 1970s with the increasing
accessibility of transportation, especially air travel,
and the arrival on the market of cheap luggage,
mass-produced and of dubious quality, made outside
Europe and the United States. Only the trunk-
making company founded by Jesse Shwayder truly
made the most of that revolution and managed its

own transformation by reaching a wider consumer market with the famous Samsonite suitcase. In England, H. J. Cave, famously one of the first modern trunk-makers in history, was recently revived, but its reach and production remain on a rather small scale. One of the very rare companies outside France with a similar destiny to that of Louis Vuitton was founded by Guccio Gucci in Italy in 1921, and went on to become the global success everybody knows today.

The predominance of French trunk-makers in the field of luxury luggage probably comes from French high society's romantic approach to travel. Whereas – in line with their reputation and lifestyle – Americans had a pragmatic take on luggage (Samsonite is a case in point, if you'll forgive the pun), French companies tried to protect their vision of travelling in style and invested in exceptional craftsmanship, as well as branching out into other luxury products such as clothing, perfumes, shoes and accessories.

French Trunks and the Transport Revolution: The New Art of Travel

The history of Parisian trunk-makers is of course linked to that of the several transportation revolutions: rail in the mid-nineteenth century, transatlantic voyages in the early twentieth and air travel in the 1920s and 1930s. In the early nineteenth century France lagged behind England, Belgium, Switzerland and Germany in infrastructure, partly because of the disastrous economic effect of the Napoleonic wars. The railway network consequently took longer to build there than in neighbouring countries. The lines were at first modest, a few dozen kilometres, usually between neighbouring cities (Montpellier and Sète, Paris and Versailles) or linking mining or industrial towns to waterways.

A turning point came in 1859 with the creation of six different rail companies. Twenty years later, in 1879, the famous Plan Freycinet launched public projects that aimed to create almost 9,000 km (more than 5,500 miles) of new railway track, to bring the total to more than 38,000 km (23,500 miles). It included the creation of 181 new lines, some just

1.5 km (1 mile) long, others extending over 200 km (120 miles). It was almost completed at the dawn of the Great War.

This hectic period, in which travelling habits changed radically, gave rise to such great companies as La Malle Bernard in 1846, Moynat in 1849, Goyard in 1853 (formerly Maison Martin, founded in 1792) and Louis Vuitton in 1854. As travellers' needs underwent radical change, Parisian trunk-makers rivalled one another in invention and talent to produce smaller chests, more handy and better adapted to the new conditions of transport. They came up with flat trunks, which were easier to stack in plane compartments; lighter 'English' trunks made from wicker; *malles-cabines*, which replaced the huge wardrobe trunks and could be put away under the beds of cabins; and drawer trunks, which were essentially portable pieces of furniture.

Before cars became common, in the early twentieth century, trunks were fastened to the roof of horse-drawn carriages. The widespread adoption of the motor car revolutionized the field of luggage and opened the door to many innovations. With the early limousines (whose chauffeurs still sat in an outside booth, with a small roof and a partition between them and the passengers), trunks were lodged on the roof rack or *impériale*. Later, the advent of coach cars and the disappearance of roof racks meant that trunks would be stored at the back of the car (hence the American term 'trunk', which corresponds to the British 'boot'). Moynat was then the great specialist and leader in automobile luggage, devoting entire catalogues to it, while Louis Vuitton was renowned for its flat trunks and plane trunks and Goyard specialized in sublime custom-made luggage for the elite.

A vintage Louis Vuitton trunk, with its famous patented unpickable tumbler lock, is photographed in the family mansion in Asnières-sur-Seine.

LOUIS VUITTON MALLETIER

The Most Famous French Name in the World

Louis Vuitton is a fantastic entrepreneurial success story, one of the most incredible France has ever known in terms of sheer global reach. The company, which shares its name with the man who founded it in 1854, has for many years been no longer simply a luggage- and trunk-maker's business or even a clothes and accessories business. It has become the ultimate symbol of French luxury across the world, and one of the most sought-after brands on the planet. In some places the worship of the brand is tantamount to that of a cult (in Asia, for example). The company has managed to renew itself impressively, investing with flair in such areas as ready-to-wear, accessories, watches, perfumes and even publishing, with its famous *City Guides*, which have gathered respect as genuine works of reference.

Everything seems to have been said about this icon of French luxury. Volumes have been written about its formidable history, including those published by the firm itself, such as *100 Legendary Trunks* (2010) and *The Birth of Modern Luxury* (2007). I shall therefore not attempt to relate the whole story of Louis Vuitton here, or even try to suggest a new approach to such an eminent company; it would be pointless and impossible to do in a few pages.

What I really want to do, with the help of the beautiful photographs taken by my friend Andy Julia, is to highlight what is for me the heart and backbone of this gigantic luxury group, the world-leader of its kind: its workshop in Asnières-sur-Seine, in the northern suburbs of Paris. This is the firm's historical workshop, the place where Vuitton's immense trunk-making skill is best expressed, far from the gloss of fashion shows and luxury magazines.

Louis Vuitton, which gave its initials to the world-famous group LVMH when it merged with Moët Hennessy in 1987, has become the world's biggest advertising force in luxury goods. But, at heart, it remains a maker of beautiful trunks and luggage, a top-drawer specialist in leather-work.

In an age when marketing and communication reign supreme, it is important to point out that beyond the worldwide celebrity and glamour of a brand whose influence has spread around the globe, its work is still (fortunately) based on the exceptional craft of artisans who have been recognized as the elite of their kind.

A vintage Louis Vuitton trunk with the Monogram canvas is photographed in the Vuitton family mansion in Asnières-sur-Seine.

The Fabulous Destiny of Louis Vuitton

According to corporate legend, the company's saga started during the troubled July Monarchy of 1835, when Louis Vuitton himself, then only fourteen, left his native Jura mountains for the capital city, walking the entire 400 km (250 miles) and carrying nothing but a small duffle bag. In Paris he apprenticed himself to M. Maréchal, a prominent *layetier-emballeur* with an affluent and aristocratic clientele. His shop was at 217 rue du Faubourg Saint-Honoré, where today the famous Colette boutique stands.

A *layetier-emballeur* was a member of a very special profession. *Layette* is an old French word that used to mean 'box' but whose modern meaning, 'baby clothes', has shifted to one type of content for such boxes. *Emballer* means 'to pack'. The profession entailed making customized boxes, chests and trunks to protect precious or fragile items. Packing the objects themselves was an integral part of the job, as was folding the clothes (often luxury outfits), which were costly and cumbersome, especially women's dresses. Vuitton stayed in Maréchal's employment for more than ten years,

eventually becoming senior clerk, and in 1853 Napoleon III's wife, the recently crowned Empress Eugénie, acknowledged his work by making him her main packer.

The connection between Vuitton and Empress Eugénie is probably at the root of what became the Vuitton company, for she opened the doors of the most wealthy clientele in France and abroad to the young man. Less than a year after becoming the favourite imperial packer, the young trunk-maker opened his own business, starting out with a boutique on rue Neuve des Capucines in Paris.

The Flat Trunk Revolution

The man who gave his name and initials to the greatest luxury group in the world was inspired by a British trunk-maker, H. J. Cave, who invented the Osilite trunk, lightweight and easy to stack. As early as 1854, Louis Vuitton followed in Cave's footsteps while the transport revolution was in full swing, and created a product that became his first commercial success and made his name: the flat trunk, considered by many to be the first modern piece of luggage. Instead of being curved,

The Vuitton family mansion was built in 1859 on the same site as the historical workshop, and is today a private museum.

A Louis Vuitton flat trunk of 1879: probably the first piece of luggage in the modern era.

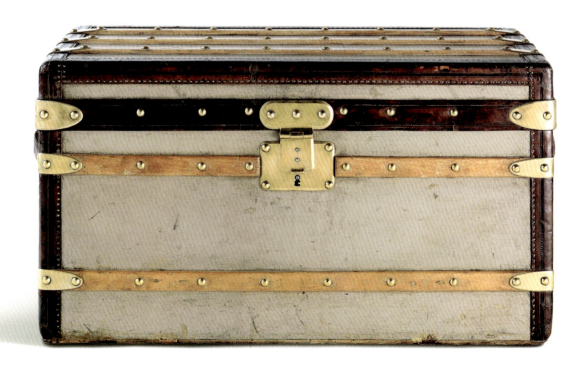

like all the trunks of the era, this trunk had a flat top. It was made of poplar wood and covered with a grey waterproof canvas, the famous Trianon canvas.

Vuitton's products were an immediate success. In 1859 he opened his own workshop in Asnières-sur-Seine, where he employed twenty trunk-makers. The workshop soon grew – to 100 in the year 1900 and 225 before the First World War – adjusting to the constant rise of the company and the continuing transport revolution. On the same plot of land Vuitton had two mansions built, one for himself and his wife, the other for his son Georges.

When Georges Vuitton took over the direction of the company in the early 1880s, it was the beginning of the trunk-maker's international, ever-increasing expansion. The first boutique abroad opened in London in 1885 before the company set out to conquer the rest of the world.

An Incredible Workshop

The peerless workshop in Asnières is not simply still in operation; it remains one of the hallowed grounds of international trunk-making, with 200 artisans working on special orders. Before visiting the historical birthplace of the Louis Vuitton group, I had a very different idea of how the workshop would be. In fact, its atmosphere is studious, even hushed – surprising for a place where you find such physical and potentially noisy activity as that of leather specialists, cabinetmakers and even locksmiths.

Only exceptional pieces are dealt with here: special orders for rich international customers. They have nothing to do with the ready-to-wear products sold by the thousand to the Asian tourists queuing in front of the sublime flagship boutique at the corner of avenue George V and avenue des Champs-Elysées. Rather, each trunk is made to measure in line with traditional methods and to

This vintage Louis Vuitton trunk features the striped canvas that is, chronologically, the second of the house's four historical canvases.

A mail trunk of 1885 in striped canvas, covered with hotel stickers.

These advertisements were published in *Vogue* in 1928 (centre left and centre right) and 1930 (left), and in 1909 in the *Salon de l'Automobile Illustré* (right).

A special 'men's trunk' of 1899, made from zinc.

Opposite

A special 'photography trunk' of 1929, in red Vuittonite canvas.

Pages 170–71

Today, in the Louis Vuitton workshop in Asnières-sur-Seine, some 200 highly skilled artisans work on special orders from all around the world.

exacting standards by highly specialized workers who are allowed to take their time in order to turn out the best possible trunks – a luxury in any manual profession today.

The workshop's team contains many artisans who have received official national awards. Some are Maîtres d'Art or Chevaliers des Arts et Lettres. They are true living treasures.

Vuitton's International Success: Bridging the Gap Between Aristocracy and Democracy

The extraordinary success of Louis Vuitton, especially since it was bought by LVMH under the leadership of Bernard Arnault, is a cause of fascination, wonder and surprise. It is hard to comprehend how a company that specialized in leather-work and trunk-making was able to conquer virtually all niches of the luxury market.

After due reflection I think I can suggest a few reasons that (I hope) should outlast the changing explanations of modern marketing specialists and commentators. Firstly, Vuitton is indisputably the heir of a true legacy of innovation. The firm was

the first to make the flat trunk popular, creating the first modern piece of luggage – that is, the first practical item that could be handled without dedicated carriers.

Secondly, Vuitton was the first to suffer modern counterfeiting, being copied by numerous competitors as early as the late nineteenth century. It responded by creating its famous monogram, one of the oldest and most eminent logos in the world, rendering it a pioneer of branding well before the advent of modern ideas of corporate identity and marketing.

Thirdly, the firm was able to understand, cater to and harness the developments of the modern era, and to do so better than any other. It thus became an important player in the field of 'democratic luxury', if I can coin such a paradoxical phrase. Ostentation may still be alive today, especially in Russia, China and the Middle East, but the luxury industry has undergone great change over the last five decades. Aristocratic ostentation has mostly given way to a more emotional approach based on a quest for better quality of life, with consumers adopting a more aesthetic attitude to their possessions. The

philosopher Gilles Lipovetsky brilliantly explained that trend in his book *Le Luxe Eternel* (2003):

> What matters now is not to challenge others but to please oneself. Pleasure is now a private thing, in line with hypermodernity. Distinction has become a narcissistic feature, not a social one. It is not about showing off, but rather about enjoying oneself in private, with goods that are loved for the power of imagination they bring.

This new 'hypermodern' trend is at the heart of contemporary luxury business, and Vuitton has been able to tackle that dimension better than other companies.

Finally, Louis Vuitton has always been able to balance the two-sided need for both modernity and eternity. When one buys a luxury object, such as a Vuitton trunk, there is a deep connection to a special sense of time. Thus, buying a Louis Vuitton piece means buying something inscribed with time, fighting the decay of things, the lack of substance.

In terms of volume and turnover, the Asnières workshop is only a drop in the ocean of Louis Vuitton's luxury empire, which boasts thirteen factories and a centre for research and development. Still, it is this one workshop that remains the backbone and heart of the company, commanding admiration and respect and lending it a sense of tradition – and possibly eternity.

Louis Vuitton's Marthe Chenal vanity case of 1926 in crocodile leather.

The patented tumbler lock was invented in 1886 by Louis and Georges Vuitton, and is still in use today in its original design.

Louis Vuitton's four historical canvas patterns, in chronological order: Trianon (1854; bottom right); the striped canvas (1872; bottom left); Damiers (1888; top right); and Monogram (1896; top left).

MOYNAT

The Renaissance of an Iconic Trunk-maker

I n 2011 Bernard Arnault, the famous French tycoon and owner of LVMH, bought the name and archive of a formerly glorious company that had folded in 1976. In doing so he gave the kiss of life to the business founded by the Parisian trunk-makers François and Octavie Coulembier in 1849 and named after their new partner, Pauline Moynat. This famous merchant who specialized in luggage and travelling paraphernalia was, legend has it, the only woman to make a name for herself in what was at the time strictly a man's world.

That the firm of Moynat should come back from the dead to claim its rightful place on the luxury market did not go unnoticed among specialists and lovers of high-end luggage, as well as competing companies who wondered about such an unexpected and cautiously handled resurrection. As a matter of fact, there was cause to wonder. The name had been completely forgotten since the 1970s, and the archives were interesting but not in any way larger than those of other baggage-makers from the rue Saint-Honoré neighbourhood. There was, therefore, a whole world to bring up to date or reinvent so as to find a new identity and, more importantly, a clientele.

In the field of luxury luggage – a Parisian niche indeed – customers are rich and loyal to their brands,

and conquering new ones is far from easy, especially in the top price range. Yet Moynat, fine company that it is, immediately made its name obvious with its born-again luggage and bags of the utmost elegance and exquisite taste. This resurgence was boosted by the talent of Ramesh Nair, a prudent and gifted Indian designer who had previously worked at Hermès.

Moynat can boast a rich record of technical innovation and design. A century and a half after its foundation, its distinct identity and aesthetic codes have been revisited by Nair with unquestionable panache.

Moynat: The Innovative Company

The beginnings of Moynat coincided with a key period in the development of the French railway. As it gained importance, this new mode of transport revolutionized people's travelling habits, and numerous trunk- and luggage-makers emerged to supply those new needs.

In the early nineteenth century, travel had been the preserve of very rich families, explorers or young British aristocrats who went on their lengthy

This vintage vanity case dates from the beginning of the twentieth century.

The Limousine attaché case is ergonomically designed to interact with the body and not hit the leg while the carrier is walking.

The Limousine briefcase, seen here in a plain black leather version, has a distinctive curved base.

Opposite

From left: The interior and exterior of Moynat's flagship, which opened in 1869 in front of the Comédie Française in Paris; Moynat's current Parisian *maison de vente* on rue Saint-Honoré.

A wicker trunk of 1873, sometimes known as the English trunk.

Moynat's automobile trunks were advertised prolifically in the 1920s.

Automobile trunks were Moynat's great speciality during the transport revolution of the early twentieth century.

Grand Tours. Those from other spheres of society rarely enjoyed travel as we know it today. The development of the railway network in France and throughout Europe opened up the possibility for more people to travel, triggering a series of innovations in the world of luggage-making.

It was not long before Moynat made a name for itself in that new and dynamic market, leaving an indelible imprint thanks to its numerous inventions. As early as 1854, François Coulembier patented a

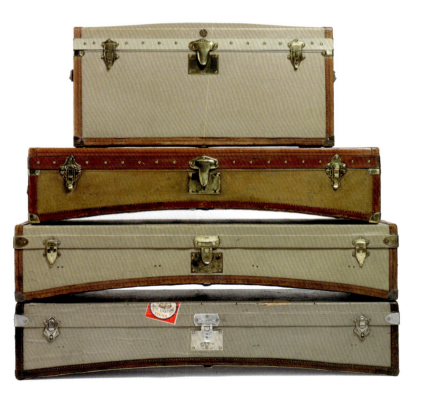

waterproof canvas coated with gutta-percha, a latex made from a tropical sap. This innovation soon became widespread and guaranteed that trunks were completely waterproof, a significant improvement.

In 1873 Moynat was also the first company to create the wicker trunk, sometimes known as the 'English' trunk. It is extremely lightweight, as the structure is made from wicker covered with leather and a gutta-percha canvas. It was the perfect answer to the new needs and rules of modern transportation. Weight restrictions (for trains and transatlantic liners, and later planes), for example, necessitated a constant quest for lightweight, robust and ergonomic luggage, and Moynat's so-called English trunk was adopted by many travellers who wished to avoid the new concept of excess baggage charges.

Over the years, numerous patents made Moynat one of the leading trunk-makers. The company garnered awards at the Universal Exhibitions in Paris in 1867, 1878, 1889 and 1900.

The Art of Automobile Travel

Moynat was the indisputable king of automobile trunks, and this house speciality became the main reason for its renown. Its numerous inventions and patents enabled it to become the leader of this booming market at the beginning of the twentieth century.

During the infancy of car travel, trunks were still lodged on top of the vehicles, as they had been on carriages. The Limousine trunks patented by Moynat had a curved base that enabled them to fit perfectly on the earliest cars' rounded roofs, improving their appearance and stability; they were

also held slightly away from the roof on rails, thus allowing air to circulate and avoiding the build-up of humidity and moisture between roof and trunk.

Later on, during the 1910s and 1920s, car trunks moved to the rear of the vehicle. These external rear trunks (*malles arrière*) were the forerunner of the modern car boot. Yet again, Moynat made a distinctive mark with its impressive rear trunks that were made to measure so as to fit the back of the car exactly. At the time, one would bring a new car to the trunk-maker after collecting it from the coachbuilder. In 1927, in a functional and aesthetic tour de force, Moynat invented side-loading cases specially for cars that had a spare tyre at the back.

Moynat's Contemporary Trunks and Luggage

In line with Moynat's record of constant progressive thinking, the new company has determined to carry on turning out original and innovative contemporary luggage, such as the 'picnic case', created to fit the front wheel of a bicycle; the Jaguar trunk, made to the measurements of an F-Type's boot; the Macaron trunk, made for the famous pastry chef Pierre Hermé; and the spectacular Breakfast trunk, a small portable kitchen made for the celebrated French chef Yannick Alléno.

For all this technical prowess and display of craftsmanship, however, it is Moynat's luggage that

Moynat keeps alive its tradition of ingenuity with unique creations such as the Macaron trunk, created for the Parisian pastry chef Pierre Hermé (above, left), and a picnic trunk crafted for a woman's bicycle (above, right).

The Moynat Holdall travel bag.

The Pauline 24h travel
bag is named after the
founder of the firm,
Pauline Moynat.

Paradis is a structured
travel bag with patented
brass angular 'bridge'
hardware on the handle.

The monogrammed Tote
bag, a patented model,
with four handles.

receives the attention of the media and customers worldwide. The secret to that lies – more than in the archives, the name or the legacy – in the man who was chosen to develop the brand's new style, the unassuming Ramesh Nair.

Nair trained at Hermès with Martin Margiela and then Jean Paul Gaultier. Although not previously a very well-known figure, he belongs to that new category of designers whose complex mission is to reinterpret, modernize and reinvent but also protect and develop a legacy or masterpiece created by someone else. To put it another way, they are artistic directors in historical houses whose remit is to be modern – to highlight the essence of the brand within the context of their own era or, as Charles Baudelaire famously put it in 1863, in the chapter 'On Modernity' in his essay *Le peintre de la vie modern, éloge de Constantin Guys* (*The painter of modern life: A tribute to Constantin Guys*), 'to capture eternity within transience':

He is looking for that quality which you must allow me to call 'modernity'; for I know of no better word to express the idea I have in mind. He makes it his business to extract from fashion whatever element it may contain of poetry within history, to distil the eternal from the transitory. . .

By 'modernity' I mean the ephemeral, the fugitive, the contingent, the half of art whose other half is the eternal and the immutable.[1]

Where other designers might have tried desperately to give an antiquated or even 'old money' look to their new creations so as to comply with the style of the house's formidable archives and the spirit of the trunk-makers of the time (and others *do* do that brilliantly), Nair took everyone by surprise. He chose the opposite line, presenting luggage that indeed took its inspiration from the house design but remained superbly understated and modern. The perfect examples are the Limousine briefcase or suitcase, whose concave base enables the carrier to walk unimpeded; the superb Holdall city bag; and the Pauline travel bag, a brilliant design that suits both men and women.

Paris and London

Since 2011 Moynat has been very cautious and gradual in its expansion, with only two splendid boutiques, on rue Saint-Honoré in Paris and on Mount Street in Mayfair, London; a few trunk shows in luxury department stores in Paris, Seoul and New York; and a gallery on Pedder Street in Hong Kong. This low-key but consistent way of developing the brand suggests a rosy future for a company that turns out some of the most beautiful and sophisticated luggage in the world. It is both a historical name and one for the future.

1. English translation by Jonathan Mayne (London, 1964), p. 224.

The Limousine, seen here in both briefcase and suitcase versions, has a curved bottom inspired by the car trunks of the 1920s and 1930s.

The Limousine briefcase photographed by Andy Julia on the famous Pont Alexandre III in Paris.

PARISIAN HAUTE PARFUMERIE

5

Page 184

A vintage bottle of
Le Troisième Homme
(The Third Man)
by Caron.

A large glass bottle of
thyme extract is ready
to be used in Caron's
perfume laboratory
near Paris.

Throughout human history, men have used fragrances, developing a complex relationship with them, whether in religious practices or purely secular contexts.

France has always been at the vanguard of this world of fleeting, subjective and symbolic nuances, and stands out as the main country for the production of upmarket perfumes.

As the researcher Caroline Plé explained perfectly in an article in 1998, fragrance-making really began to develop during the Renaissance, when the army of the French king François I fought in Italy.[1] The Italians had opened the Silk Road, and had subsequently made extensive use of spices and of the new scents from the East, becoming the first Europeans to produce scented oils. The more austere countries in Europe did not see perfume

with the same liberal eye, and did not develop it the way the Italians did. The French became the Italians' first competitors, especially as they were able to produce their own substances, unlike the Italian makers, who had to import them.

Thanks to its strategic situation near Italy and its perfect soil and climate, the town of Grasse in the south of France became the world capital of

---

1. 'Le Secteur industriel de la parfumerie' ('The French Perfume Industry'), *Revue de géographie de Lyon*, LXXIII/1 (1998), pp. 97–103.

fragrance, producing substances of a quality unmatched anywhere else. French prominence in the field of perfume-making has been steady ever since. Of course, the traditional handmade production has evolved, and mass production has been a feature of the industry since the 1920s. Perfume has also become a key element in the 'democratization' of luxury, as most haute couture companies, especially in Paris, now distribute their own fragrances.

Perfume is now a mass-produced luxury product made in state-of-the-art factories, but there are still several historical houses that keep an artisanal approach, such as Guerlain and Caron, two illustrious Parisian perfumers of exceptional character that have produced some of the most famous men's fragrances in the world.

The facade of Caron's Left Bank boutique, on the boulevard Saint-Germain in Paris.

Guerlain's historical Parisian flagship has been at 68 avenue des Champs-Elysées since 1914.

GUERLAIN

Message in a Bottle

In 1836 the writer Honoré de Balzac ordered from Pierre-François-Pascal Guerlain a perfume that would be conducive to writing his famous novel *César Birotteau* (1837), whose main character is a perfumer and social climber. In 1919 Serge Diaghilev decided that, before every performance, the Bolshoi Theatre's red curtain should be sprayed with his favourite fragrance, Mitsouko by Jacques Guerlain, who went on to create another perfume, Coque d'Or, specially for the director of the Ballets Russes. And in 1933 Jacques Guerlain created Vol de Nuit (Night Flight) as a tribute to his friend the writer and pilot Antoine de Saint-Exupéry.

Guerlain, the French icon of perfume, is one of the world's oldest houses specializing in perfume and beauty products. It has earned great respect and plaudits for its timeless fragrances and divine potions for women, but has also produced beautiful scents for men. The history of the firm's production of these celebrated fragrances, many of which – Vétiver, Habit Rouge, Mouchoir de Monsieur, among others – are now considered classics, is rich in fascinating and intimate detail.

Thierry Wasser, the 'nose' of the house, is the fifth of the creative master-perfumers of the Guerlain dynasty. He is the first who is not related by blood

to the family, but since he was chosen in 2008 by Jean-Paul Guerlain as the rightful heir of that lineage, Wasser has become the natural and legitimate spokesman of his adoptive family. The way he talks about the firm's exemplary olfactory legacy confirms that, sometimes, the bonds of the heart and spirit can be as strong as blood ties:

Saying that a perfume is for men or women has always seemed a bit strange to me – smell is such a personal experience. Of course we have to guide our customers through our range of products, but you would be surprised to know how many men secretly wear *Shalimar or Jicky*. . .Although Guerlain has an international reputation for women's fragrances, the various perfumers of the family have always been intimately associated with the distinguished gentlemen of their times. It has inspired them to develop major innovations in perfume: Vétiver was Jean-Paul Guerlain's very first fragrance in 1959 and it has become an absolute classic,

Thierry Wasser and Jean-Paul Guerlain.

Le Mouchoir de Monsieur (The Bridegroom's Handkerchief) and Voilette de Madame (The Lady's Hat Veil), seen here in their original *escargot* (snail) flacons, were specially created by Jacques Guerlain for a friend's wedding.

as well as Habit Rouge, an original fragrance created in 1965. It was the first oriental perfume for men.

Luxury houses throughout the world are trying at all costs to promote their legacies, and the least scrupulous make much of very remote connections with history. In that context, claiming that each perfume created by the noble line of Guerlain noses was linked to personal experience (often affairs of the heart) might sound like a horrible marketing gimmick, but the truth is that in the case of the Guerlain family, it's just plain understatement.

The names chosen by the prolific Jacques Guerlain at the beginning of the twentieth century sound like the catalogue of an impressionist painter – Jardin de mon Curé (The Vicar's Garden) and Après l'Ondée (After the Rain), for example, or the incredible confession to a mysterious woman, Voilà pourquoi j'aimais Rosine (This is Why I Loved Rosine). Another such, Mouchoir de Monsieur (The Bridegroom's Handkerchief), was created in 1904 for the wedding of one of Jacques's friends, at a time when men's fragrances did not enjoy widespread popularity. He also concocted a perfume for the bride, Voilette de Madame (The Lady's Hat Veil). Mouchoir de Monsieur came a few years after Jicky (1889), the first truly contemporary fragrance, and shared the same spirit. It is now regarded as the first men's perfume.

In 1914, to celebrate the opening of what was to become the firm's historical boutique at 68 avenue des Champs-Elysées, Jacques created Parfum des Champs-Elysées. It was presented in a tortoise-shaped bottle – a sarcastic nod to Charles Mewès, the architect (and also designer of the Ritz Hotel), who had been very slow to finish the shop.

When Jacques's grandson Jean-Paul Guerlain explains how his very first fragrance, Vétiver, is a reminiscence of his old childhood gardener, who smoked brown tobacco, it is clearly not one of those prettified stories made up by unimaginative corporate marketing services. There is evidently a Guerlain way of doing things, and, in creating fragrances, its artists have always found inspiration in real life and emotion, without heeding marketing trends and targets.

It seems to me that perfumers – especially those of the Guerlain family – are possessed of a rare and exceptional gift: the ability to give shape to an emotion, a fleeting gaze, a sweet memory. Of course, in French, *sentir* (to smell) and *ressentir* (to feel) are not only very similar but also often used interchangeably. Guerlain's olfactory legacy is the expression of hundreds of personal stories that gave birth to thousands of formulae, conscientiously written down and meticulously kept in the secret Book of Formulae by Wasser, their new guardian.

Pierre-François-Pascal Guerlain: By Appointment to European Royalty

The connection of each Guerlain fragrance to a specific person should not be surprising, since the house's main practice was creating bespoke perfumes for the rich clientele of the Hôtel Meurice on the rue de Rivoli, where Pierre-François-Pascal Guerlain first established his boutique in 1828. From his position as 'Fragrance and Vinegar Maker' inside the luxury hotel (vinegar-based lotions were very much in use at the time), he moved to rue de la Paix in 1840. News spread, and soon everybody in the upper classes knew about his skill in creating fragrances that subtly expressed a personality or ambiance.

Le Mouchoir de Monsieur in its current *abeilles* (bees) flacon.

Pierre-François-Pascal
Guerlain (left) and
Aimé Guerlain (right).

European royalty took note of Guerlain's perfumes, skincare creams and other beauty products. His famous Strawberry Cream was favoured by 'Sisi', Empress Elisabeth of Austria, and he counted among his faithful customers no less a figure than Alexander II (for whom Pierre-François-Pascal's son Aimé created Cologne Russe in 1880) and Alexander III of Russia, and Alfonso XIII of Spain, who inspired his Eau Hégémonienne in 1890. In 1853, at the peak of his fame and artistry, Guerlain composed Eau de Cologne Impériale for Princess Eugénie, Napoléon III's wife, and became the emperor's official perfumer.

Aimé Guerlain: Impressionist Perfumer

Aimé Guerlain would contribute in a crucial way to the family's olfactory edifice. Whereas his father had been a master at mixing floral, animalic and woody essences to create his perfumes, Aimé was a chemist, traveller and explorer who brought something radically new to modern perfumery: abstraction. He was one of the first perfumers to use synthetic molecules, a revolution in the art of perfumery, and a radical new approach to imagining fragrances.

In 1889 Aimé created his masterpiece, Jicky. He composed the fragrance while under the spell of a young British woman, and through it he brought the art of perfume-making to a previously unknown level by using synthetic molecules for the first time. The era of floral, animalic or woody representationalist scents was giving way to olfactory impressionism: for the first time, a perfumer was seeking not to reproduce the atmosphere of gardens and vegetation but rather to translate emotions and impressions.

Jacques Guerlain: The Nose of the Century

Aimé's nephew Jacques has been hailed as one of the greatest noses of the twentieth century, and possibly of the entire history of perfume-making. During sixty years at the head of the family empire, he created more than 400 fragrances, some of them emblems of modern perfumery.

In 1912, in line with the revolution initiated by his uncle, he created a masterpiece of olfactory impressionism: L'Heure Bleue (Twilight). This innovative fragrance reproduced the impressions of his favourite time of day, the fleeting moment when it is not yet dark and the sky is tinged with an evocative touch of blue. It is a sunset kind of fragrance, like a nod to Monet, of whose work Jacques was particularly fond.

In 1925 Jacques created Shalimar, the first women's fragrance with an oriental touch. It marked the beginning of international success for the house of Guerlain, and remains among

the great classics of modern perfumery. Shalimar was of great importance for Guerlain, and not just for the international praise it garnered, then as now. It was the first fragrance for which Jacques used his famous 'Guerlinade' ('Guerlain Mix'). This concoction of six natural ingredients he loved to combine became the house's olfactory signature: a distinctly recognizable one of rose, jasmine, iris, vanilla, coumarin and bergamot orange.

Thierry Wasser explains the company's approach to synthetic perfumery:

We were among the first to use synthetic extracts in our formulas, for both women and men, as with Jicky in 1889 and Mouchoir de Monsieur in 1904. It opened up a wider range of creative possibilities. But we have always used a lot of natural substances, too. . .The 'Guerlinade' that Jacques and Jean-Paul were so fond of using over decades is not only the olfactory signature of our house but also suggests a very original approach to perfume-making, where you limit yourself to short formulae with few ingredients. It is much more difficult to compose a fragrance with short formulae than to create one with a formula three pages long and a mass of extracts and ingredients. Trying to strike a fragile balance between very powerful ingredients and very short formulae enabled Guerlain to turn pleasant fragrances into real olfactory statements.

In perfumery, as in literature, it seems one should always tell a story with simple sentences. . .

Jacques continued to contribute to the history of Guerlain until he passed it on to his grandson Jean-Paul in 1955, some eight years before his death. He remains a figure of modern perfumery, a prolific and creative artist who made a tremendous mark.

Jean-Paul Guerlain: The Creator of Vétiver and Habit Rouge

Jean-Paul Guerlain likewise proved himself a daring and prolific artist, creating such classic fragrances for women as Chamade and Samsara. His contribution to the field of men's fragrances, however, was also a major one.

In fact, Jean-Paul started out with a men's perfume, Vétiver, after working from a very early age with his grandfather. Vétiver, a tropical

plant the root of which is distilled to produce a very subtle woody essence, lent its name to a fragrance that ranks among the great classics of modern men's perfumes.

At the time it was created, in the early 1960s, very few beauty products were designed exclusively for men, apart from aftershave balms. Vétiver was a first foray into that field, and heralded a new era for men's perfumes and beauty products.

In 1965 Jean-Paul struck again with one of the most original fragrances ever, Habit Rouge (Red Jacket). It was composed as a tribute to horse-riding, a world he knows well, and is regarded as the very first oriental fragrance for men. Its refreshing, intense notes of lemon, orange and bergamot can be surprising, even dismaying or shocking at first, but they gradually fade into something warm and oriental with hints of smoke, leather and vanilla. This radical fragrance is certainly a love-it-or-hate-it perfume. A typical Guerlain concoction with its short formula and Guerlinade-based mix, it stands out with a strong character.

For the next forty years Jean-Paul relentlessly pursued the family's work, bringing international success to the business. Scores of new fragrances

Jacques Guerlain with his nephew Jean-Paul Guerlain.

Shalimar, created in 1925, in a contemporary *abeilles* flacon.

Vétiver and Habit Rouge are two men's fragrances by Guerlain that have become classics.

came on to the market, the range of care and beauty products kept developing and Guerlain became a truly international company.

Chamade (1969), Parure (1974), Eau de Guerlain (1975) and Samsara (1989) entered the Parisian hall of fame of fragrances, and Terracotta (1984), the first moisturizing and bronzing powder, became immensely successful in both Europe and the United States. New skincare creams, powders and make-up products were greeted with unanimous enthusiasm by women all over the world for their quality and extreme sophistication. In 1994 the company joined the LVMH group portfolio, the epitome of Parisian style. In 2008, fifty years after creating Vétiver and without an heir, Jean-Paul passed on the Book of Formulae to a Swiss perfumer whom he chose personally: Thierry Wasser.

Jean-Paul Guerlain would be more than a mere predecessor to Wasser, and it can be seen as a respectful nod to the older master that Wasser started out with a men's fragrance, Guerlain Homme, a woody, sparklingly fresh scent that heralded a new era for *maison* Guerlain.

Thierry Wasser: The Spiritual Son

Thierry Wasser trained as a botanist and worked as a perfumer for two great names, Givaudan and Firmenich, before he became Guerlain's in-house nose in 2008. As the first perfumer from outside the family, he struck up a strong relationship with his mentor, Jean-Paul Guerlain, being aware that although Guerlain had the organization and methods of a luxury company, transmission could not boil down to merely technical detail of formulae and routines:

Every week since I started my work here, I have always spent half a day with Jean-Paul so he can hand me down the immense olfactory legacy of Guerlain – it cannot be reduced to a few formulae.

Guerlain has unique expertise, but the main thing is the special spirit of the firm. All the perfumers in that lineage were strong characters who always followed their instincts, using their own lives, their experience with people, their love stories, their affairs and passions, their whims and fancies as the very substance of their creations. It is vital for me to be able to spend time with the

last of these giants to keep that spirit alive. It is a unique and sincere approach to perfume in a world where consumer research tends to take precedence over artistry.

When one thinks of it, it is a true miracle that such an intuitive and unwritten creative approach should have survived through generations of perfumers and produced such a consistent and recognizable style. But there is an explanation.

The Book of Formulae: The Perfumer and the Scrivener

When Wasser showed me the handwritten secrets in Guerlain's Book of Formulae, I was immediately reminded of copyist monks patiently transmitting words down through the centuries. These pages are filled with the scrawl of the past. They detail the ingredients, the doses and even the intervals for the inclusion of each substance and extract. The old-fashioned script holds an obvious fascination despite its obscurity for the lay reader.

What is even more fascinating is that all the perfumers of the family were as much creators as copyists. They were inventors, but the process simultaneously involved writing things down, copying, improving, commenting and transmitting a work that spans decades, its author not a single person but a whole family.

Until the invention of printing, scriveners did not simply copy the documents with which they had been entrusted, but also duplicated, transmitted and otherwise kept them alive, to such an extent that sometimes the original author's name was lost. Such a comparison could apply to artisans working for many old firms of classic men's style, who have tried to pass on their craft and expand their stylistic legacy, whether through garment patterns or shoe lasts. But in the case of fine perfume, and especially with Guerlain, this is not just a simile, since fragrances are fundamentally about mixing, adding, punctuating, deleting, refining and accenting. As an art form perfumery is very close to the conscientious approach of the knowledgeable copyist trying to respect a text as well as adding to it so that it is passed on. Wasser is the fifth artist and 'copyist' of a huge masterwork, still alive and unique almost 200 years after it was begun.

Thierry Wasser works with Guerlain's secret Book of Formulae. This handwritten book contains all the formulae for Guerlain's creations, and has been preserved and transmitted from perfumer to perfumer for five generations.

L'Homme Idéal (The Ideal Man) by Guerlain was released in 2014.

L'Eau Boisée (Scent of Wood) was created by Thierry Wasser in 2012.

CARON

The Maverick Fragrance-maker

I am not the best-looking man in the world. And yet, they say I have a lot of charm. That's because of my secret weapon. . . Pour un Homme, by Caron.

In 1972 the great Serge Gainsbourg wrote the lyrics and composed the music for a song he sang with his muse, the British actress and singer Jane Birkin. It was used as an advertisement for his favourite fragrance, Pour un Homme de Caron.

A certified maverick, inveterate smoker, militant boozer and ironic dandy, Gainsbourg was also an artistic genius and the proponent of a philosophy of decadence. In the 1970s he was the musical equivalent of the perfumer Caron: a rebellious spirit asserting his right to freedom of speech in a world whose tastes and spirits were increasingly stifled by mind-numbing standardization – all in the name of progress, of course.

Later on, during the 1980s, hundreds of heavily branded but ordinary and characterless colognes invaded a market suddenly swamped by advertising hype. The luxury goods industry and famous brands from the worlds of fashion, jewelry, ready-to-wear and sportswear discovered the world of flashy perfume, and the promise of easy money gave rise to the invasion of all-powerful, logo-obsessed marketing.

During that period, every brand had its own fragrance in an attempt to attract customers, who were responding like an easily duped herd. Marketing had become a technique that served

to delude the masses, enabling the most insipid perfume to be presented as a 'creative experience'.

Gainsbourg's wild lifestyle meant that he died all too soon, as he had decided he would, but his songs remain alive in the French collective mind. Only now, more than two decades after his death, are we starting to realize that Gainsbourg was not just a provocative and amoral rebel, a drunk entertainer, but an artist whose very life advocated freedom of choice and of expression.

In 2000 Richard Fraysse, the talented and enlightened perfumer who has worked for decades with Patrick Alès, Caron's illustrious and innovative owner, created L'Anarchiste. The name itself was a nod, possibly involuntary, to the deceased songwriter. As a matter of fact, the fragrance is unique, not least – in marketing terms, for a start – because of its shocking name, a true hymn to freedom, proclaiming its strong personality and standing out conspicuously in the morass of a market overwhelmed with vapid products.

Caron has always been the odd one out among perfumers, staying faithful to its roots despite hardship and tribulations, never yielding to fads and trends or the whims and fancies of marketing experts. As early as the late 1910s Félicie

Caron's luxurious boutique is on the boulevard Saint-Germain on Paris's Left Bank.

Wampouille, the muse of Caron's founder, Ernest Daltroff, said she believed more in the virtues of word of mouth than in advertising, and she decided that Caron perfumes should be sold only in Caron boutiques. This kind of freedom, in word and action, was often at odds with the evolving trends of the luxury market, but it was this very attitude that enabled Caron to become such an original company, a true jewel of French perfume.

After a period of great uncertainty, during which Caron was passed like a hot potato from one hand to another (including the supermarket group Cora), the golden egg of Parisian perfume eventually landed in good hands. They were those of Patrick Alès, an apparently clairvoyant entrepreneur, endearing and atypical, who did more than just restore the past glory of a company that was almost a century old.

Alès has been responsible for putting Caron back on track, resuming the course of this unique company, whose creations kept shaking things up, and offering men and women fragrances with a strong character. This is the extraordinary and very touching world of Caron.

Ernest Daltroff and Félicie Wampouille: Love and Fragrances

Ernest Léon René Lucien Daltroff was born on 17 November 1867 at his parents' house in Sainte-Cécile in Bourgogne. His father, Louis, came from Russia, and was Head of Division at the local railway in Paray-le-Monial. The rest of his family was part of the Jewish elite in Paris.

Very early in his life, Ernest travelled around the world and developed a gift for recognizing and memorizing scents. Following his personal taste, he decided to become a chemist and perfumer,

and in 1902, with his brother, he bought a small haberdashery-perfumery on rue Rossini in Paris.

The pair's reason for choosing the name Caron for their budding business remains shrouded in mystery. Some specialists say it was a tribute to a famous acrobat of the time; others claim it as the name of the previous owner, one Anne-Marie Caron. Whatever the case, Caron is a simple, typically French-sounding name, and it became a historical symbol of French perfumery.

The enterprising and optimistic Daltroff brothers also bought a small upstairs office in the renowned rue de la Paix, as well as a small perfume factory called Emilia in Asnières-sur-Seine, in the suburbs of Paris. This was where they started their creative experiments with fragrances. The year 1906 is an important one in Caron's history, as it was when the brothers were joined by Félicie Wampouille, a young designer whose role at first was to help Ernest to create bottles and packaging for the fledgling business. Wampouille, with whom he soon fell madly in love, dedicated her entire life to the company. She ran the business until 1962, long after the death of its founder (which occurred in 1941 in the United States, after he fled anti-Semitism in France in 1939).

Ernest and Félicie rapidly produced original fragrances whose evocative names met with great success, both in France and abroad. Their first triumphs came with Chantecler in 1906, Narcisse Noir (Black Narcissus) in 1911, L'Infini (Infinity) in 1912 and Ravissement (Rapture) in 1913. Caron consequently opened a boutique and a small factory in New York in 1923.

In 1916, while a generation of men was fighting in the trenches, Caron launched N'Aimez que Moi (Love Only Me), a fragrance given by many soldiers

Le Tabac Blond is a distinctive fragrance created in 1919 by Caron in homage to the US soldiers who introduced the famous Virginian tobacco to Europe. It evokes the sweetness of Virginia tobacco smoke, without containing any tobacco extract.

to their wives or girlfriends in the hope that they would behave while their men went through their terrible ordeal. Three years later, as an homage to the US soldiers who had introduced the famous Virginian tobacco to Europe, Caron launched Le Tabac Blond (Light Tobacco). This fragrance (which is still produced by Caron) was intended for men, at a time when they used only cologne or handkerchief perfumes (such as the famous Mouchoir de Monsieur, created a few years earlier by Jacques Guerlain). The story goes that it was actually women – the newly emancipated flappers sporting men's clothes – who adopted the new fragrance.

Le Tabac Blond was among the first fragrances to use leather as a dominant tone. It is still part of Caron's catalogue, and keeps pleasing men and women alike. Soft, sweet and complex, it was part of the first generation of 'impressionistic' fragrances – like Guerlain's Jicky – trying to avoid replicating nature's scents, and instead evoked the feeling of sweetness of Virginia tobacco smoke, all without the tiniest extract of tobacco.

Pour un Homme de Caron: An Eternal Masterpiece

The Daltroff-Wampouille duo delivered its masterpiece in 1934. Daltroff loved lavender; Wampouille loved vanilla. Since he was madly in love with her, Daltroff attempted the strange conjunction of both aromas, producing a legendary and prestigious fragrance that is still one of Caron's biggest sellers.

In Pour un Homme two supposedly antithetical scents were merged. As my son Greg Jacomet – a great nose, fragrance lover and perfume specialist for *The Rake* magazine – comments on the *Parisian Gentleman* website:

Matching two such polar opposites requires nuance and finesse in order to become more than just a gimmick. Or an olfactory disaster. Pour un Homme succeeds in an almost troubling fashion. The balance is so perfect that at times it becomes hard to tell the lavender and the vanilla apart as they dance wrapped around each other, revealing unforeseen qualities in both.

When vanilla has the upper hand, the lavender makes itself known like a breeze over the French Riviera, gently stinging your nostrils. When the lavender has the upper hand, its bold scent is gently tempered by the warm and well-rounded vanilla, which in turn acquires a slight herbal edge. And the two play, discuss, change seats, but always with great discretion, while you've got your back turned.

Pour un Homme de Caron leads the way for men's fragrances. It was an overnight success, and remains a major reference today.

The Alès and Fraysse Partnership

In 1998 Patrick Alès, who wished to acquire a perfume company, was moved by the story of Caron, an emblem of the French art of perfume that was losing its soul after too many thoughtless buyouts. He talked to the owner, who agreed to sell it to him. Perfumes are made with plants and essential oils, and the Alès Group was then among the leading buyers of oils in the world, especially for the famous Phytosolba products, renowned for their solely plant-based formulae.

Richard Fraysse comes from a great family of perfumers. This famous nose is the grandson of the creator of Yardley's Lavender and the son of Jeanne Lanvin's nose, who famously

Clockwise from top left: Ambergris is a very precious substance formed in the stomach of the cachalot whale and used in high perfumery as a fixative or fragrance enhancer; a relic of ancient perfumery, these testicles from a Tibetan musk deer contain a substance whose use and sale was forbidden in the 1980s, along with the hunting of the animal. Musk was used mainly as a fixative, and the development of synthetic alternatives means that it is no longer used; Pour un Homme de Caron (1934), a vibrant dialogue between lavender and vanilla, is one of the best-known men's perfumes in the world; dried lavender flowers form the base of Pour un Homme.

Overleaf

The perfume organ is traditionally where a perfumer works on the composition of a fragrance, mixing and weighing the different extracts and ingredients. This one is Richard Fraysse's at Caron. However, today most of this work is now carried out with modern equipment.

composed Arpège (Arpeggio) for the great Parisian haute couture house.

In 2000, two years after Alès had bought Caron, he and Fraysse produced a fragrance for men whose name and character were to be a milestone for contemporary perfume: L'Anarchiste. After almost forty years of aimlessness and doubt since the death of Félicie Wampouille in 1967, Caron was back with a fragrance unlike any other.

Ordo ab Chao: *L'Anarchiste* as seen by Greg Jacomet

Caron is a house unlike any other. Whether one likes it or not is almost irrelevant: the venerable Parisian institution has never caved in to trends, nor has it ever rested on the laurels of its past achievements.

Caron is an uncompromising house that deals in the avant-garde. Its successive noses have created an impressive range of innovative and almost niche perfumes with enthusiasm and talent. Pour un Homme de Caron of 1934, the first perfume exclusively marketed to men, is the historical jewel to its proverbial crown.

Richard Fraysse, the current house nose and creator of L'Anarchiste, upholds a simple assertion: Caron has not lost its flame nor its audacity over the years. L'Anarchiste is proof that it is still possible in today's masculine market – a market drowning under gallons upon gallons of vapid scents – to release something unique.

Secreted in a superb copper-plated bottle – a singular mix between a Prohibition-era whisky flask and an Art Deco sculpture – lurks one of the most indefinable and unique fragrances of its generation. The opening notes are powerful, almost overwhelmingly so. Chaos ensues, in a whirlwind of orange, mint, vetiver and wood (most likely cedarwood). Then the most volatile notes evaporate, and confusion settles in. I say 'confusion', because that's what I perceived from the look I got when someone stopped me in the street to ask what scent I was wearing. I could read in her face a mixture of curiosity and utter bewilderment, which was absolutely justified. I could swear I can smell metallic notes in L'Anarchiste, but maybe it's because of the copper on the bottle. . .Still, there might very well be a spot of rust hidden away behind the mixture of spices (prominently clove and cinnamon) that comes in a warm gust of wind to balance the freshness of the top notes. Close to the skin, the base is musky with perhaps a hint of iodine.

Whatever L'Anarchiste contains, the interaction between the different notes is so complex that everyone seems to smell whatever it is they think they smell. Olfactory solipsism, if you will. Some people have even reported smelling notes of blood. . .But for all its complexity, L'Anarchiste is surprisingly coherent; a perfume both warm and fresh, slightly dirty, very woody and very masculine.

True to its style, Caron has indeed released a unique perfume in L'Anarchiste. It is an ambivalent fragrance, both warm and fresh, which mixes familiar notes with some very experimental associations. It is at heart a very urban and cosmopolitan perfume. It establishes its own precedent, and that quality alone makes it one of the most contemporary and original perfumes on the market today. In Caron's L'Anarchiste, order is born from chaos.

G. J.

Richard Fraysse is the third generation of a family of 'noses'. His grandfather created Lavender for Yardley and his father created Arpège (Arpeggio) for Jeanne Lanvin. His son is already working with him at Caron.

Romain Alès, the president of Caron, with Richard Fraysse, the in-house perfumer.

The Maverick Fragrance-maker

The story of Caron is not an ordinary one, let alone an artificial tale cooked up by marketing services attempting to give an impression of authenticity. It is a story about men and women with strong convictions, a story of passion, tough calls and tough breaks, success and defeat, respect for elders and freedom. Ernest Daltroff and then Félicie Wampouille, who ran the house until 1962, were the cornerstones of that great company, and both Patrick Alès and his son Romain seem to be their worthy and natural heirs.

At a time when companies tend to invent a past for themselves, or when financial groups buy out historical companies with an eye on short-term profit rather than on preserving craft, it is always a relief to chance upon a company where men and women, rather than spreadsheets or soulless strategic planning committees, influence the decisions, sometimes against the grain of economic rules.

In 1998 Alès saved Caron from the dreaded fate of becoming a banal commodity, a standardized product. Today his son, a dynamic and passionate man, is in charge, and Romain's profoundly honest dedication to preserving and developing the legacy of the company is nothing less than admirable. The care the Alès family has taken of the Caron legacy is in many ways reminiscent of the Colban family's preservation of Charvet.

When Romain Alès speaks of Caron, of L'Anarchiste, of Pour un Homme or of the delicate Yuzu (another composition by Fraysse), it is as if those fragrances had been part of his family for centuries, rather than being the result of an acquisition by his father's group only about fifteen years ago. It is his way of protecting and developing one of the most original olfactory legacies in the world, enabling thousands of people *not* to be like everyone else – contrary to most modern marketing. I am pretty sure that, somewhere, Serge Gainsbourg is nodding in approval.

Caron's men's collection of perfumes in their original flacons. (From left to right:) Pour un Homme de Caron, Yatagan, Le Troisième Homme, L'Anarchiste, L'Impact Pour un Homme and Yuzu.

L'Anarchiste (The Anarchist), one of the unsung heroes of male perfumery and probably one of the most distinctive men's perfumes on the market, is photographed in its original copper flacon.

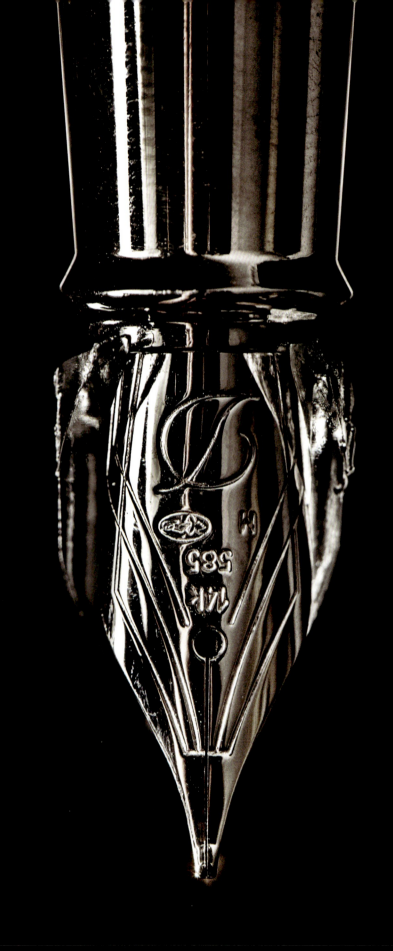

GENTLEMEN'S REQUISITES

6

Page 214

A fountain pen by
S. T. Dupont.

A timepiece and
precious cufflinks by
Mellerio dits Meller,
one of the most
ancient jewelry houses
in the world.

Since about 2010, with the widespread renewal of men's interest in their personal appearance and elegance, the market for accessories has picked up and expanded. Many small companies are becoming specialists, sometimes even ultra-specialists, in one type of item (for instance shops focusing on necktie jewelry) or accessory (such as outlets devoted to socks made from high-end fabrics).

It has even become difficult to find one's way around, given the overabundant offering that features the best and the worst, in terms of both quality and aesthetics.

With so many marketing experts wallowing in the commercial tumult that vaunts the merits of 'the elegant gentleman' *ad nauseam*, I have chosen to focus on just two quintessentially Parisian institutions: Cartier, a name synonymous with Parisian luxury thanks to the firm's contribution to the renown of French jewelry worldwide; and S. T. Dupont, which remains the most famous maker and distributor of lighters in the world.

Among the small Parisian boutiques that should not be missed is Howard's, where superior ties are designed, made and sold in a single shop on rue d'Amsterdam. Another intriguing boutique is Mes Chaussettes Rouges (now a famous name), whose two founders pioneered the return of knee-high socks into the wardrobe of elegant gentlemen after having the idea of distributing the socks sported by Vatican clergymen, including the famous red socks worn by the pope.

In another field, even more upmarket, it is impossible to miss the lovely, discreet company Mellerio dits Meller, a master jeweller on rue de

la Paix. This is one of the oldest of its kind, dating back as far as 1614, and is part of the exclusive organization Les Hénokiens, a not-for-profit association of family businesses that have been in existence for more than 200 years throughout the world. Other members of that famously quiet organization include such legends as Vitale Barberis Canonico, the oldest weaver in the world, and Piacenza, the cashmere specialist.

Mellerio dits Meller is still run by a descendant of the original family, which was granted the privilege of 'carrying cut crystal, trinkets and other small goods between said town of Paris and elsewhere throughout the kingdom without let or hindrance by any person' by Queen Marie de' Medici of France in 1613. Peddlers of 'cut crystal'

soon came to be called 'jewellers'. Mellerio offers superb accessories for men, particularly cufflinks and several truly original timepieces. It is a fine Parisian company, very much lacking in exposure, but one that any elegant gentleman ought to visit.

Cufflinks in white gold and mother-of-pearl by Mellerio dits Meller.

Mellerio dits Meller's distinctive timepieces and cufflinks are sold from its wonderful boutique (bottom right) at 9 rue de la Paix, Paris.

CARTIER

Jeweller to Kings, King of Jewelry

In 2007 Hans Nadelhoffer, a jewelry specialist of worldwide renown, wrote a magnificent book soberly entitled *Cartier* for Thames & Hudson (incidentally, the publisher of the book you're reading, as you may have noticed). During three years of research, the writer (who is also an expert for Christie's in Geneva) was allowed unlimited access to the archives of one of the world's most famous jewellers.

When I visited the wonderful Cartier boutique on rue de la Paix in Paris for this book, I heard a lot about Mr Nadelhoffer, whose publication is considered by many at Cartier to be the house bible. Imagine my embarrassment when I read his precise and erudite book, more than 350 pages long, when I had decided that I would write a simple chapter about a jeweller bearing one of the most famous French names in the world, the very embodiment of Parisian luxury.

Since I am not an expert in timepieces and have avoided in all my published work, whether on paper or online, this highly specialized subject about which so many people are passionate, I found myself in a pickle, to say the least. How could I – in a book called *The Parisian Gentleman* – not talk about such a distinguished house, which Edward VII himself had called 'Jeweller to Kings, King of Jewelry'? Given my ambition, how could I ignore the immense contribution of a company whose stylistic boldness in jewelry and watchmaking in the early twentieth century was celebrated by all the kingly courts of Europe and the world? How could I not write about one of the greatest suppliers of luxury accessories to the greatest men in history – and luxury on so huge a scale?

As luck (or rather, my friends at Cartier) would have it, I found my way out of this predicament thanks to the literally providential (and very private) exhibition 'Cartier's Man', which took place in spring 2014. Things *do* work themselves out, if you can believe it. The exhibition was held in a quiet, refined private drawing room upstairs in the Cartier building on rue de la Paix, and didn't – or so it seems – benefit from any photographic coverage.

Alexander I of Yugoslavia bought these platinum Cartier cufflinks with emeralds and sapphires in 1929, and presented them to King Carl II of Romania.

This Cartier tie pin in gold, platinum, enamel and rose-cut diamonds was made by special order in 1917. It was ordered by HRH Crown Prince Alexander of Serbia, who was assassinated by a Macedonian separatist in Marseille on 9 October 1934.

This Cartier tie pin of 1907 is made from platinum and gold and set with rose-cut diamonds and *calibré*-cut rubies.

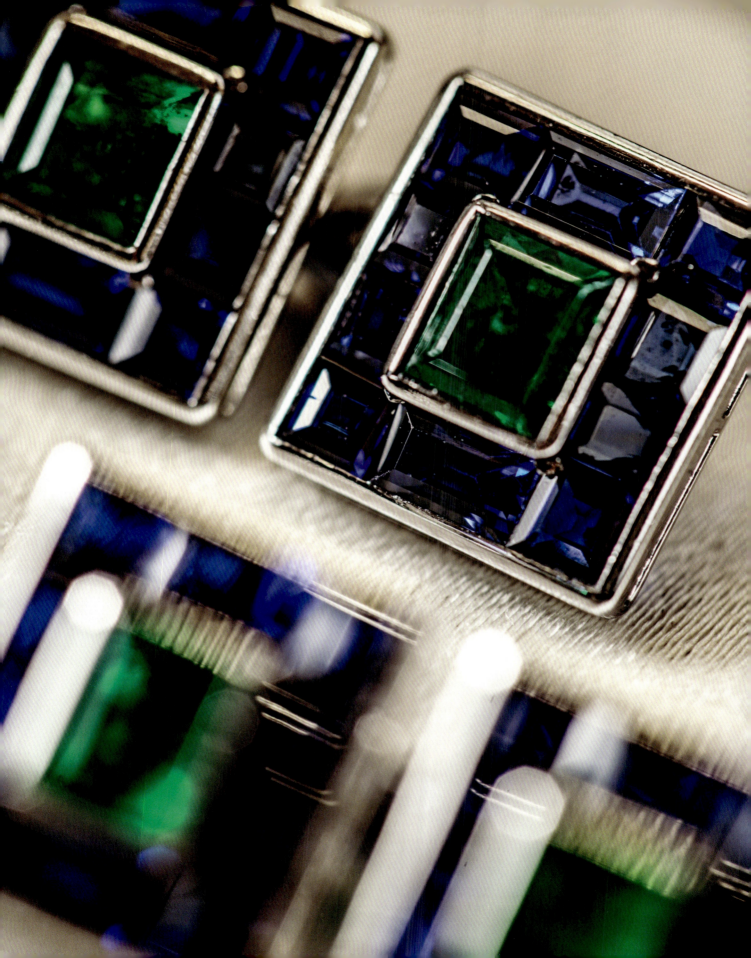

Opposite

Cartier brushes from 1966 in 9-carat gold are set with *calibré*-cut lapis lazuli cabochons and bear the monogram 'SG' for the famous British–American Hollywood actor Stewart Granger.

A letter-opener by Cartier Paris from 1913 is made from gold with a nephrite blade and bears four sapphire cabochons with onyx and black enamel. It was sold to the Aga Khan.

These gold Cartier cufflinks dating from 1945–47 include a compass and watch.

Rose-cut diamonds, a striped pattern of black and white enamel and an onyx seal distinguish this Cartier telescopic mechanical pencil from about 1912. The pattern called *pékin* in Cartier ledgers refers to narrow, parallel stripes of enamel, alluding to Pekin-weave fabrics in which glossy stripes alternate with matte ones.

This page

This gold double pocket magnifying glass by Cartier Paris dating from about 1912 also bears the striped pattern of gold and white enamel known as *pékin*. It is monogrammed 'GW'.

A pocket knife by Cartier Paris from about 1905 is made from gold and steel with striped decoration (*pékin*) of white and translucent green enamel on a *guilloché* ground.

Cartier Paris Guillotine cigar cutter, *c.* 1907, in gold with translucent grey-blue enamel over *guilloché* ground, white enamel and four pearl buttons.

The Russian cigarette case made by Cartier Paris in 1913 with gold sapphire cabochons (thumb-pieces) and white enamel has on the right-hand side a compartment for matches with striking surface.

Opposite

This 14-carat gold belt buckle by Cartier New York (1950) incorporates a watch with a movement by the Round Concord Watch Co., rhodium plating, seventeen jewels, Swiss lever escapement, monometallic balance and Breguet balance spring. It was also known as a golfer's watch. As early as the 1920s several watchmakers began offering watches that were worn on the belt, to protect the movement from the shock of the wrist as the wearer swung a golf club.

In it were brought together for the first time a careful selection of historical items for men, of great artistic value. Far from the usual exhibitions featuring exceptional watches and jewelry for women, which are at the heart of Cartier's craft and identity, this presentation was, I am glad to say, entirely dedicated to pieces for men. Many were rare items and most had been produced for particular individuals.

Tie pins, cigarette holders, cufflinks, pocket knives, clothes brushes, money clips, lighters, cigar cutters, belt buckles and writing instruments were therefore offered to the camera of Andy Julia. Tribute could thus be paid to Cartier's very great contribution to men's paraphernalia, a contribution that is not as well recognized as the firm's role in watchmaking, despite its significant importance for men's elegance. It was a more than welcome exhibition, and we have tried to immortalize these exceptional objects for this book as a fitting homage to a house that has contributed greatly to the brilliance of French luxury across the world.

This cigarette case in the shape of an envelope was a special order from Cartier London in 1932. In polished and engraved 9-carat gold with red, white and black enamel, it was ordered by Sir Winston Churchill for the twenty-first birthday of his son Randolph. Knowing of the young man's absent-mindedness, Churchill wittily asked Cartier to engrave Randolph's address on it, in facsimile handwriting. When the Cartier collection acquired this piece, the seller stated that during a trip to Egypt, Randolph had offered it to King Farouk, who had expressed his admiration.

This gold cigarette case with black enamel by Cartier Paris in 1922 is engraved on the inside cover: *Paris, / le 5 décembre 1922 / Bonne chance / André Citroën / Paris / le 16 Février 1923 / Bravo!!* [Paris, 5 December 1922 / Good luck / André Citroën / Paris, 16 February 1923 / Bravo!!]. It features a 'Kodak system' opening, a shutter mechanism that is released by pressing the two push-pieces on the sides. This case was sold to André Citroën (1878–1935), who launched the car firm that still bears his name. Like Henry Ford, he made cars more widely accessible and was the first European manufacturer to mass-produce a single model, the Type A. Also innovative when it came to publicity and marketing, Citroën organized and promoted an automotive crossing of the Sahara Desert from Algiers to Timbuktu. The inscription here commemorates this trans-African trek, which took place between December 1922 and February 1923.

Black enamel and 14-carat gold billfold with watch by Cartier New York, dating from about 1933. The watch pivots to protect the dial when the billfold is carried in a pocket.

A cigarette case from 1912 in silver, green gold and pink gold by Cartier Paris, with one sapphire cabochon (push-piece). It was sold to Willis McCormick, president of Queen Aviation. The inside of the case is engraved with the signatures of approximately thirty figures related to the birth of aviation, including Maurice Chevillard, Igo Etrich, Jacques Mortane, Perreyor, Alberto Santos-Dumont, Jules Védrines, Gabriel Voisin, Roland Garros, Raymond Saulnier and Jacques Schneider.

This gold Cartier pocket watch with
white enamel decoration (*pékin*), pearls
and rose-cut diamonds incorporates a
chain and matchbox (not seen) and was
made in about 1910.

S. T. DUPONT

'You'll Be a Man, My Son'

If you're looking for a quintessentially French name, Dupont is among the first to come to mind.

When I was a teenager in the mid-1970s, being offered a Dupont lighter was a significant event that marked your coming of age. If your father or grandfather handed down his own Dupont lighter, it was even more poignant. Such an event meant that you had become an adult, and were no longer obliged to submit to the authority of your family. Epochal moments like this separate the boys from the men, and if you had a Dupont lighter in your pocket, there was no doubt that you were stepping into the world of real men.

Of course, this was also another era, when smoking was almost compulsory if you were an adult and your first packet of cigarettes was usually bought for you by your own father. But the Dupont lighter was not just about smoking. I knew several young men who did not smoke and who were still offered a Dupont lighter by their parents for their eighteenth birthday or to celebrate their graduation.

There is nothing surprising about that: the Dupont lighter was always among the rare and precious everyday objects whose appeal and message were much more important than their function. For many middle-class young men like me, it was also the first expensive article they'd ever actually owned.

This lighter is still one of the most sought-after in the world. What makes it so special is that it represents important manufacturing secrets. (Think of that famous opening 'cling', which has made the lighter legendary.) It was introduced in 1952 as a butane-fuelled lighter, and has remained the enduring flagship of the brand against a sea of troubles, for – quite apart from the recent rise of disposable lighters and the ban on tobacco advertising – the company's history has not been plain sailing.

As a matter of fact, even though S. T. Dupont remains one of the French Republic's greatest suppliers of state gifts to official guests, the brand has been through various owners and branched out (not always successfully) on more than one occasion, before eventually going back to its original identity. With this last move it reasserted its essence, that of a luxury company with craftsmanship at its core, creating exceptional goods in its own factory in Faverges in the French Alps.

The Ligne 2 lighter by S. T. Dupont is the most famous lighter in the world, with its inimitable 'cling' at the opening of the lid.

The Art of Crossing the Atlantic

S. T. Dupont was founded in 1876 by Simon Tissot Dupont, a manufacturer of leather goods by trade and former photographer to Napoleon III. Dupont was quick to grasp that the new transatlantic liners would very shortly transform the art of travel among the high society.

At the beginning of the twentieth century, the founder's two sons, André and Lucien Dupont, steered the company in the exclusive direction of luggage, trunks and travel cases, vanity cases and other travelling paraphernalia. In 1919, straight after the First World War, the Duponts decided to open their own factory in Faverges. In order to be able to produce such fine luggage, combining craftsmanship and ingenuity, the factory incorporated no less than seventeen specialized trades, including goldsmiths and silversmiths, engravers, brush-makers and experts in *guilloché*, lacquer, crystal, enamel – and, of course, leather.

During the 1920s, the weight of luggage became a real problem for high-society travellers owing to new safety regulations on board ocean liners, and so there was an urgent need for trunks and bags made from new, lighter materials. S. T. Dupont therefore embarked on a new adventure, discovering Chinese lacquer, a rare material whose manufacture carried extraordinary technical demands, the mastery of which would become a prized speciality of the house.

Replacing enamel and wood with lacquer and metal alloys enabled a weight loss of 40 per cent, and spread the firm's name among the global elite. Kings and princes, emperors and maharajas all over the world became loyal and enthusiastic clients, for S. T. Dupont was able to satisfy the most extravagant requests and meet the most elaborate challenges, working with such precious materials as gold, diamonds, mother-of-pearl, tortoiseshell, Chinese lacquer and alligator skin.

Minaudières and Lighters for the Maharaja's Concubines

In 1938 the maharaja of Patiala in northern India, a ruler known for his unrestrained love of beautiful women, ordered one hundred *minaudières* to offer to his favourite concubines. A *minaudière* is a small case or clutch bag in which to carry everything a lady might need during a reception or walk: make-up, lotions, pocket mirror and compact, for example, as well as tortoiseshell comb, cigarette holder, timepiece, purse or dance-card. It was a

A luxurious vanity case by S. T. Dupont, dating from about 1900.

very popular accessory during the 1930s. Devoid of any handle, it was carried like a book and, according to women's magazines of the time, was supposed to bring about 'a revolution in the composure of ladies' during social engagements.

The maharaja requested from Dupont that each *minaudière* be provided with a small, solid-gold lighter. This exceptional order took three years to complete, and, just before the Second World War, it changed the course of the brand forever. The first Dupont lighter had been created.

The Most Famous Lighter in the World

With the gradual decline of traditional high society in Europe and the United States, this new speciality for the firm led to a complete restructure that turned out to be providential. From then on, S. T. Dupont made fewer and fewer pieces of luggage, except for the occasional request, such as the order in 1947 of President Vincent Auriol's gift of a travel case for the wedding of Queen Elizabeth to Prince Philip.

At the end of the war S. T. Dupont launched a petrol-fuelled lighter; its first gas-fuelled lighter, with a solid brass body, was launched in 1952. The first version was already an exceptional piece of work; wonderfully balanced and understated, it also had a clever and durable mechanism. Using solid brass resulted in a more robust lighter, and since it was cast in a single piece without a reservoir there could be no leakage. Brass also offered unprecedented possibilities for *guilloché* and other sophisticated finishes. It was an enormous success, and seemed to be adopted by the whole world.

The Hollywood jet set simply adored it, and it was proudly sported by such ambassadors as Humphrey Bogart, Marilyn Monroe and Audrey Hepburn. It became Alfred Hitchcock's, Pablo Picasso's and Andy Warhol's exclusive lighter.

In 1977 the famous jeweller Jean Dinh Van reworked the design and proportions of the lighter to produce the S. T. Dupont Ligne 2 ,which remains the ultimate Dupont lighter for collectors and lighter-lovers all over the world. Fine-tuned to perfection using the golden ratio, the Ligne 2 was finer and less stubby than its illustrious predecessor. Once again, the firm's clients were enthusiastic. And yet there was a rub, an unexpected and unheard-of glitch: the opening of the lid was much too noisy, the opening 'cling' too loud and clear. The Dupont brothers tried to get rid of it – to no avail.

The 'Cling' Made it King

While S. T. Dupont was desperately trying to remove the defect from its new lighter, its customers simply fell in love with this charming noise. Far from being considered a fault, the unique sound quickly became famous and was embraced by customers who regarded it as a sign of belonging to a certain class of people, the select few. Opening a Dupont lighter publicly, letting out that recognizable 'cling', will get you noticed: you don't have to speak or even be seen. Buyers in Japan and Hong Kong were smitten. They loved the noise, and, realizing that each lighter had its own particular sound, they started choosing their own signature 'cling'.

The Dupont brothers did not simply drop any attempt to remove the formerly unwelcome

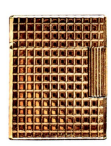

The S. T. Dupont Classique ball pen was created in 1973 for Jackie Kennedy. This ultra-slim pen, which is still distributed today, became a classic and remains the only ballpoint pen to be exhibited at the Museum of Modern Art in New York.

A series of vintage S. T. Dupont Ligne 1 and Ligne 2 lighters from different periods and in various materials and finishes.

sound; they even carried out research to keep it as consistent as possible. They worked with the greatest precision on the connection between body, lid, hinge and overall design in order to achieve the highly complex operation of reproducing a particular pitch mechanically. In the Faverges factory, a trained sound expert checks that the sound of each lighter conforms to the Dupont signature pitch. Counterfeiters have attempted to copy this trade secret, but with very poor results so far, despite sophisticated mechanisms, including hammers and bells.

S. T. Dupont lighters come in many different versions, and some have a staunchly contemporary appearance, but they always comply with the high standards of quality, sturdiness and style that have come to define this accessory. With its original 'cling', the Ligne 2 is still among the house bestsellers, while a huge market for second-hand lighters and collectors' items has been blossoming online. The Dupont lighter is still as hot as ever.

Jackie Kennedy Onassis and her Dupont Pen

Just as the Maharaja of Patiala had changed the company's course in 1938, so another illustrious client inspired S. T. Dupont's second revolution. John Fitzgerald Kennedy's widow, now remarried to the famous Greek shipping magnate Aristotle Onassis, was so enamoured with her lighter that in 1973 she asked S. T. Dupont to create a pen to match it. The firm's creative genius was to extend the roller part of the lighter (the small metal mechanism that acts as a switch when flicked with the thumb) to become the body of the pen, inventing a beautifully slim implement.

With its slender shape and delightful writing flow, this pen was also easy to hold. It became a classic – the name, Classique, *was* well chosen – and is exhibited at the Museum of Modern Art in New York.

As the lighter had done before it, the Classique conquered the world and propelled the company into the market of collectible pens. S. T. Dupont held this course with several collections of pens, the excellence of which has been universally acknowledged. The writing pleasure they bring is most obvious with such pens as the Olympio, the Défi (the fountain-pen version of which is among the best of its kind today), the Liberté and, most recently, the President.

Back to its Roots

A surprising series of twists and turns followed for S. T. Dupont. When it joined the trend for disposable lighters at the beginning of the 1970s with its Cricket brand, it was bought by the Gillette group. It was then sold in 1987 to the Hong Kong business mogul Dickson Poon, an important player in luxury retailing.

Throughout the years S. T. Dupont continued to assert considerable influence in the market for luxury lighters and collectible pens, but it strayed needlessly into such uncharted territory as ready-to-wear clothing, a venture that resulted in the firm's biggest failure, in the early twenty-first century. It caused great problems for a brand that had hitherto been synonymous with French flair.

In 2006 the former head of Givenchy, the charismatic Alain Crevet, stepped in and introduced radical change, breathing new life into the company and in the process saving it. His strategy was simple, yet ambitious: to go back to the company's roots and focus on its historical craftsmanship so as to win back the place it deserved as a Parisian luxury brand.

The strategy paid off handsomely. The company became profitable once more and used the momentum to relaunch the founding craft of S. T. Dupont, its original *raison d'être* – luggage and luxury leather goods.

The Faverges factory, which had closed in 2008 after a fire, reopened. It is still the main hub for the company, and employs a dazzling array of top-notch craftsmen. The very rare art of lacquer is among the traditional crafts for which S. T. Dupont is renowned across the globe.

Sophistication and Simplicity: S. T. Dupont as the Epitome of Parisian Style

Although S. T. Dupont changed direction and sometimes even drifted into dubious territory, its style has stayed alive, enduring with remarkable panache the changes in fashion and society. That style is one of a kind. Straightforward and powerful aesthetics imply that each piece in the catalogue is unique. S. T. Dupont's approach sums up what I believe to be the essence of Parisian style: an apparent simplicity that reveals true sophistication. That might also be the very definition of luxury.

Even among the greatest brands, very few have managed the tour de force of establishing not one but two legendary pieces in the Parisian luxury hall of fame. S. T. Dupont's two iconic twentieth-century pieces – the Ligne 1 and Ligne 2 lighters and the Classique pen – have both become a world-class reference point of classic design.

With this exceptional legacy, its beautiful factory and its mastery of matchless crafts, Dupont has chosen to focus on its roots. It has everything that is required to keep the wonder going.

A Ligne 2 lighter with shield and diamond head decoration in yellow gold, and finished in yellow gold.

Ligne 2 lighters with shield in Chinese lacquer and palladium (below, left) and red Chinese lacquer decoration (below), both finished in palladium.

ONE-OF-A-KIND HOUSES

7

T

he last chapter of a book that took me no less than eighteen months of hard work and many visits is devoted – as it should be – to the houses that I consider personally to be unique.

These three nonpareil firms, all of them on a human scale – in other words, small businesses – could of course have fitted into the first six chapters of the book. The incredible made-to-measure spectacles of Bonnet or the sublime pocket squares of Simonnot-Godard, for example, would not have been out of place next to Cartier and S. T. Dupont in the chapter about men's requisites. As for Marc Guyot, even if he is not a tailor in the strict sense of the word as we use it in this book, not even the most exacting of my dedicated readers would have been offended to see his name in the first chapter, given the acutely personal vision he has of men's style and the truly original contribution he makes to current sartorial debates. And yet I have insisted on setting aside a special chapter for these firms, for, despite their differences,

they have in common that their size may be small but their influence is huge.

Bonnet is the only company in the world to own, quite legally, a large stock of turtle-shell, and, more importantly, one of the last to master the technique of this very demanding material. I have a particular fondness for Benjamin and Gersende Simonnot, not only because of their unflinching tenacity in preserving and developing the family business, but also because they have brought back into style an accessory that had completely fallen into disuse: the pocket square. Finally, Marc Guyot deserves much more recognition than he has for being a contemporary designer of huge import. His thorough understanding and brilliant reinterpretation of classic men's style from the 1930s and 1940s are without parallel in the world today.

An ensemble by
Marc Guyot.

From top: The facade
of the Bonnet boutique
workshop in a typically
Parisian *passage*; plaques
of buffalo horn; two pairs
of spectacles in progress
at the Bonnet atelier.

Overleaf

A Simonnot-Godard
handkerchief,
with its distinctive
hand-rolled hem.

Inside Marc Guyot's small,
hidden boutique in Paris —
a paradise for lovers of old
tweeds and vintage fabrics.

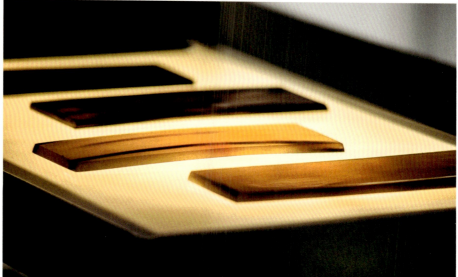

MAISON BONNET

Let There Be Light

Maison Bonnet of Paris is the only spectacle-maker in the world to produce handcrafted bespoke turtle-shell frames. The trade in this fascinating material has been strictly regulated since the Washington Convention of 1973, and it is now impossible to obtain turtle-shell legally unless the stock was accumulated before that date. Very few companies possess such a rare treasure or have been allowed by local authorities to market it.

Christian Bonnet is one of the last working turtle-shell specialists, making Maison Bonnet a peerless workshop. And yet Bonnet's mastery of turtle-shell is only one side of its uniqueness. Its true originality lies in its approach to eyewear as part of a gentleman's personal style, an approach very similar to that of a bespoke tailor or bootmaker.

At a time when 'bespoke' has become the sacred buzzword of the merchandizing gods through the agency of marketing managers who have only a very loose understanding of what it truly means, it is refreshing to chance upon a company that satisfies all the expectations of connoisseurs in the field of real bespoke service – complete customization, unique craftsmanship, luxury materials (buffalo horn and turtle-shell) and astonishingly beautiful handcrafted goods.

When I visited the Bonnet workshop for the first time, for the purpose of researching this book, I did not know what to expect, as I still had a very old-fashioned vision of turtle-shell based largely on my grandfather's lovely combs. I could not see the difference between a spectacle-maker and a run-of-the-mill optician. Some of the latter claim to be *visagistes* (beauty customizing specialists) and sell 'branded' glasses or, even worse, 'designer' spectacles at ridiculous prices. I did not grasp that while an optician will talk about sight correction and frames, an eyewear expert like Bonnet devotes itself to letting the light work its magic. It really isn't the same world at all.

Bespoke Eyewear

Franck Bonnet, Christian's eldest son, is a charming and passionate middle-aged man with an obsession: when he meets someone for the first time, he can't help but visualize in his mind's eye what kind of glasses would suit them best. It has become second nature, a sort of uncontrollable impulse that makes him immediately estimate your temporal space and discuss the contrasts of your face or the nature of your nose bridge. I've met people like that before. For instance, my tailor, Lorenzo Cifonelli, seems

An 'extra-blond' pair of turtle-shell spectacles.

to be affected by the same instinct. He will screw up his eyes to check the technical details of your suit whenever he sees you, no matter what the circumstances.

Indeed, the analogy with tailoring could continue. When I stepped into Bonnet's cosy boutique-cum-workshop in a picturesque dead-end near the Palais Royal, I noticed the same atmosphere that I feel at my tailor's or my bootmaker's. The coloured charts on the walls display cellulose acetate, horn and turtle-shell rather than leather or fabrics, but the bespoke spirit is present in every detail: measurement of the face and discussion about one's sartorial preferences and lifestyle, about the choice of material and shape, about prototyping and fittings.

At Bonnet's there is simply no ready-to-wear, not even sunglasses. The hundreds of models on display in the small showroom where the lights are kept low are only suggestions, designed to help the customers to devise models that will suit their faces with the assistance of the eyewear specialist. This is real bespoke: glasses crafted by hand, one piece at a time.

The Last of the Mohicans

Bonnet is very much the Charvet of luxury eyewear, a sort of economic aberration and industrial anomaly. Until the 1980s, the market for glasses was still a 'medical' speciality, and the market for sunglasses in its infancy. Traditional workshops were still dominant, especially those in Morez, a tiny town in the mountains of Jura and the capital city of French spectacle-makers.

In the mid-1980s logos took over the world, and eyewear was touched by this global phenomenon. Dozens and soon hundreds of brands hailing from the worlds of fashion, sport and jewelry started producing glasses, flooding the market with poor-quality products adorned with gaudy and splashy logos. Most traditional makers did not survive the new trends, and one shop after another was closed.

Faced with a difficult situation and the rise of mass marketing in the discreet world of traditional spectacle-makers, Christian Bonnet – who had taken over the company from his father in 1980 – decided that he would stand his ground. He remained committed to the idea that there was still room for high-quality spectacles in the morass of logos. Building on his unique craftsmanship in luxury

materials (mainly turtle-shell), he decided to keep calm and carry on making the most beautiful glasses in the world. This strategy enabled his firm to keep its head above water while an overwhelming wave of marketing aggression was threatening to destroy the whole profession.

This bold manner of taking charge reminds me of the forward-looking move made by Denis Colban in the 1970s and 1980s at Charvet. Like Christian Bonnet, Colban chose to resist the siren call of ready-to-wear and mass marketing, preferring to offer exceptional products, thus raising rather than lowering the bar.

Thirty years on, the world of men's style is rediscovering the virtues of craftsmanship. More and more gentlemen want to free themselves from mass-marketed logo-stamped products and turn to traditional crafts. It seems that Christian Bonnet was right after all. His firm now enjoys international praise and attention, and its products are admired everywhere for their unswerving excellence.

Down Through the Years

The Bonnet business has been handed down from father to son for four generations in a story that starts in the 1930s. Alfred Bonnet was a spectacle-maker who specialized in gold and turtle-shell in his workshop in Morez.

Alfred's son Robert followed in his father's footsteps and plied the same trade in two famous companies, first Achard and then Boidot, where he

Franck Bonnet is from the fourth generation of this family of bespoke eyewear-makers.

The Jacques Chirac model in cherry turtle-shell was originally made specially for the former French president, who led France between 1995 and 2008.

became head of the factory. In 1950 he left to found his own company, specializing in bespoke eyewear and luxury materials, including the turtle-shell that would become the house speciality. Robert's precious creations bewitched high society, and his enterprise quickly met with tremendous success as crowned heads, writers, politicians, businessmen and artists made his name in the small world of luxury eyewear.

Robert's son Christian received early training in the difficult and challenging art of bespoke turtle-shell spectacles, and this disciplined profession became his passion. At only fourteen he studied at the Institut d'Optique on boulevard Pasteur in Paris, and he was later blessed with the opportunity of working with the last great masters of turtle-shell, Jacques Rameau and François Mandon, who passed on a precious legacy of skills and tools as well as shell stocks. The workshop in Sens, Burgundy, where Christian Bonnet operates is still the heart of the company and the repository of a unique craft. He was even awarded the title Maître d'Art by the French Ministry of Culture in 2000.

Christian's son Franck joined the company at the age of eighteen, and his younger brother Steven

recently joined as well. It was Franck's impulse, however, that gave a boost to the business and brought it out of its underground position into the limelight.

New Materials

Since the stock of turtle-shell is dwindling inexorably and there is no way of renewing it, Franck Bonnet decided in 2009 to apply the company's craft to new materials such as water buffalo's or ram's horn and, more recently, cellulose acetate, which enables total freedom in terms of colour. Far from forsaking the family's craft, he pursued it, bringing bespoke glasses to more customers and thus revealing the brand to the world.

Working with more affordable materials has opened up new possibilities for the future, but it has been developed in accordance with the spirit and methods of Bonnet. Even when using a more common material, between six and thirty hours are still necessary to produce a pair of spectacles by hand. The shaping and polishing require the same care whether the material is acetate, horn or shell.

Letting the Light Shine Through: The Bonnet Touch

Choosing a pair of glasses is a complicated and far from intuitive process. If making the decision alone one runs the risk of a big mistake. Glasses have become more than just a medical device. Spectacles are now regarded as an element of style for men, and a way to express one's vision of oneself.

In his seminal book *Dressing the Man: Mastering the Art of Permanent Fashion* (2002), the great theoretician of contemporary men's style Alan Flusser gives a masterful demonstration of a core idea: if one's style is carefully thought through, the goal is to set off one's face and certainly not one's suit or shoes, however perfect they may be. Another way to say it, in imitation of George 'Beau' Brummell, is that it's the man who should receive all the attention, not the clothes.

In his excellent treatise, Flusser also broaches a topic that is rarely discussed by so-called experts: the relationship between the colour and contrasts of one's complexion and the colour of one's clothes. He shows with flamboyant clarity that only certain colours or hues can really highlight certain types of complexion. It is thus essential for a man (or woman) to know about those colours so that their face will always be seen in as good a light as possible.

This theory is given a new dimension at Bonnet. Developing Flusser's theme, Bonnet's approach aims to let light through the spectacle frame, the facets of which must be carefully shaped and polished with that goal in mind. Taming the light is at the heart of Bonnet's modus operandi. The outcome *is* stunning, as I can testify, having witnessed extraordinary results in the beautiful boutique.

'Blessed are the crackpots, for they let the light through', as the great French screenwriter Michel Audiard said. I don't know if this is a crackpot family, but I do know that Christian, Franck and Steven Bonnet really shine with all the beautiful light they create.

MARC GUYOT

The Wild Child of Parisian Style

'I am not above anything, or underneath. I am simply elsewhere', said the nineteenth-century writer Jules Barbey D'Aurevilly when asked about his legendary wild style and rebellious spirit. Such a notion also applies perfectly to the work, spirit and character of Marc Guyot, the wild child of men's style in Paris and certainly one of the most influential figures in the field, as well as one of the most endearing, in France and anywhere else.

Guyot is the proud owner of two lovely Parisian boutiques that bear his name, in the narrow rue Pasquier, near the place de la Madeleine. He is certainly opinionated:

I am not a tailor, I am a designer. I have my own stylistic vision and that's what I impose on my customers. If someone does not like my style, so be it. Frankly, I don't care about all the so-called made-to-measure suits on offer on the market. Those people can even claim to be bespoke tailors. It's none of my business. I don't deal in suits and shoes. I deal in Marc Guyot.

During the last decade, the booming and agitated world of men's style has been prey to all manner of seductive enterprises to attract customers – but Guyot hasn't followed the trend.

Marc Guyot started out as a simple shop assistant in menswear, because he felt that was his calling – against the advice of his parents, who wanted him to be 'someone' (that is, a lawyer or a doctor). Since climbing the ladder of the profession and becoming his own boss, he has always stood his ground, imposing his very personal vision of men's style whatever the pressure of fads and fashion or other short-lived whims.

Guyot has strong convictions and character and is a man of great culture. After travelling the world and meeting all the most famous figures of the business, I can personally testify that he is one of the world's greatest connoisseurs of all things sartorial. He is also the kind of person who will readily share his encyclopaedic knowledge of men's style throughout history with his friends and clients.

But be warned: if you're looking for a mundane grey or blue business suit, you will be disappointed. There *are* blue and grey suits on rue Pasquier, but they will have an hourglass bowing at the waist, 32 centimetre (12½-inch) vents, slanted pockets, Parisian lapel notches and a whole lot of other

Marc Guyot is photographed by Andy Julia in front of one of his boutiques in Paris.

details that will make the wearer stand out in a crowd. Guyot is about men's style, not simply clothing. You either love it or hate it.

In the small historical boutique in the rue Pasquier, one can spend idle hours with a mammoth cigar and a Port Ellen single malt (preferably from the Lost Distilleries collection) talking about the pattern of a Donegal tweed from the 1950s, marvelling at the sheen of a four-ply cashmere, extolling the virtues of a shirt with French seams, studying the loose nonchalance of a *manica camicia* ('shirt-sleeve') shoulder structure or the impeccable channelled Goodyear welt of a shoe. It's heaven for sartorial connoisseurs and amateurs – a small Disneyland, with cigars and spirits to boot.

We live in a time of standardization and control. Authorities, political parties, scholars and 'educational' institutions spout laws, rules and other well-meaning ordinances to keep us from eating and drinking too much or smoking at all, to prescribe 'responsible' behaviour and to instruct us how to dress so as not to offend others with too rakish a personal style. In that context, entering one of Guyot's boutiques seems tantamount to an act of resistance in the face of insistent norms that aim to smooth out unconventional thinking or behaviour. Guyot's lair is a haven of freedom and flair: a breath of fresh air in a suffocating world.

The Apparel Arts *Spirit Lives –* in Paris

The famous *Apparel Arts* magazine is the forerunner to *Gentleman's Quarterly* (*GQ*). It was launched in the 1930s and was originally aimed solely at men's clothing professionals. The pictures were so gorgeous that, according to legend, clients used to pilfer copies of the magazine from their tailors. In any event, *Apparel Arts* served to foster people's sartorial education and develop exquisite taste in classic men's style.

Having realized that there was a keen readership for this professional fashion journal, the editor-in-chief launched a new version in 1933 for the general public, entitled *Esquire*. The Esquire group published *Apparel Arts* until 1957, then renamed it *Gentleman's Quarterly* in 1958 and *GQ* in 1967. *GQ* was acquired by the Condé Nast group in 1983, thus becoming the main competitor of – you guessed it – *Esquire*.

Although *Apparel Arts* is no longer published, original issues are still sought after by connoisseurs and collectors. Its popularity was thanks to the genius artists Douglas Hurd and Laurence Fellows, the latter of whom became an icon among men's clothing enthusiasts. Although these two illustrators were then unknown to the public, they were in fact the first major arbiters of men's style in an era free of the marketing pressure and trend programmes that contemporary designers seem obliged to obey, even at the cost of their souls and the free expression of their talent.

Marc Guyot, whose flair and daredevil approach have become famous in Paris, is a direct heir to the

Guyot's French–American style is very distinctive, as these jackets show.

Fellows legacy. In 1995, as he was looking for a name for his men's collections, he even patented the name 'Apparel Arts', which, strangely enough, had not only been forgotten by the public but had also fallen through the cracks of copyright property. Guyot did not just use the name of the glorious magazine, however; he was also faithful to its spirit, re-creating in a small street in the 8th arrondissement a whole world that seems to spring straight from the imaginative inkwells of Fellows and Hurd, as if the 1930s, that golden age of men's elegance, were back in style.

Rap, Tweed and Bespoke Shirts

Marc Guyot was only fourteen when he was bitten by the sartorial bug and infected with the virus of personal style, which would develop into an obsession that would become his calling. In his own words:

'It all started with rap and skateboards and a friend's father who brought back from the States Off the Wall Vans for me. What was already important to me was to have the best of anything. It was all very selfish. I started wearing tartan trousers, Pringle of Scotland jumpers and Alden tasselled loafers – at sixteen I could already tell that for each article, there was good and there was better. As early as eighteen I had no use for ready-to-wear, and I moved on to bespoke. Since I was never satisfied with the tailors' work, I started designing my own patterns and buying my fabrics in England. I went to Turnbull & Asser in London to have my own bespoke shirts made. My sartorial education was completed in a flash. It dovetailed with the music I was listening to at the time, rap or the Style Council, Bryan Ferry, etc. It was a very rebellious thing and it enabled me to escape from conformity, something I've always found horrible.

The fledgling designer was discovering his own idols. In the early 1980s, a time when young French people spent their weekends watching action films, Guyot became infatuated by vintage American flicks in black and white featuring Fred Astaire, Gene

The famous 1930s fashion illustrator Laurence Fellows is one of Guyot's greatest sources of inspiration.

Overleaf

Two ensembles in pure Guyot style: a mix of 1930s American style and French flair.

Kelly, Humphrey Bogart, Gregory Peck and Joseph Cotten – all paragons of elegance and style.

At twenty Guyot abandoned his studies to devote himself to his passion full time:

At that time, my suits were bespoke and handmade. I had had my own lasts made and so I was wearing my own bespoke shoes. I would wear only my Edward Green shoes when it rained or snowed. As an increasing number of my friends wanted to dress like me, I referred them to my tailors, but they were never quite happy with the results: the suits were well done but without that special touch, that extra ingredient. And so I started accompanying them to fine-tune the patterns. That's when I understood that I needed to have my own business and create my own clothing.

I've been working along those lines for sixteen years, and if I suddenly stopped I wouldn't know where to buy my clothes. I'm glad that many people like what I do, but it was initially selfishness that prompted me to start all that – I was trying to create clothes for myself.

After working as a shop assistant and then shop manager, Guyot opened a boutique with a partner in 1995 before starting his own business on rue Pasquier in 1999, bringing back the spirit of *Apparel Arts* and attracting a regular crowd of faithful fans.

Not Just a Style: A Sartorial World

Spending time at Guyot's is a unique experience that no other place – not even the most reputable – can rival. Guyot is known for his perfect taste as a bold dresser. His boutique is in line with that reputation, and you can be sure you won't forget your first visit.

The two shops facing each other on rue Pasquier are decorated with illustrations by Laurence Fellows. Rolls of vintage fabrics from illustrious deadstocks (Harrisons of Edinburgh or Schofield & Smith) are stacked in a corner, and crocodile shoes sit lazily on an old patinated button-back leather couch next to a superb Norfolk jacket in Chilean linen. The atmosphere is surprising and creative, refined and very winning. Unlike many boutiques, where the assistants are stiff, where every detail is carefully designed by hired experts and where clothes are displayed according to an artificial marketing

concept, Guyot's shops are arranged simply, artlessly and haphazardly to accommodate the many regular customers who appreciate that special cosy feeling.

The genius of Guyot lies not so much in his ability to design clothes, shoes and accessories unlike any others, as in the way he has brought back a whole sartorial world. One would not be surprised if Laurence Fellows himself popped up in Guyot's boutique, or if some fashionable gentleman from the 1930s, the kind who spent his summers in Palm Beach with his family, strolled leisurely in. It is a place suspended in time, a celebration of a sartorial golden era.

Flouting Convention

When I first shook hands with Guyot, a few years ago, I thought he was a cross between Tintin, Gianni Agnelli and Fred Astaire:

Choosing your clothes is a way of expressing yourself. It should be a personal statement. When I wear knickerbockers or red tartan I do not take other people's judgments into account. You have to free yourself from that. You cannot be a slave to other people's judgment if you want to be truly elegant. The act of donning clothes is a personal pleasure. Connoisseurs will recognize one another in the street at a single glance; there's no need to say anything. It's like a game. You find that in Italy, and with Africans and Japanese people as well. Not in France any more. The way they dress in France is for their status to be acknowledged, but then it's pointless, because so few people really know the codes. For the most part, they're very ignorant.

You may not like it, but I sincerely believe that even in America and England people are more open-minded than in France. They don't walk around judging people according to what they wear. It's important to free yourself from people's judgment because that's when you break new ground. But before you fool around with the rules, you must know them by heart.

Take note of Guyot's name, for this colourful character – a true hedonist and sartorial wizard – may well gain international prominence as people slowly forgo ready-made thinking. As Glenn O'Brien wrote in the preface to *I Am Dandy: The Return of the Elegant Gentleman* (2013), 'A man who steps out of uniform is a hero, in his own way. To look different wilfully takes courage, and the highest form of courage is to reveal oneself fully, to express one's inner condition to the world with eloquence.' Thanks to Guyot, many Parisian gentlemen now have an ally in the attempt to reveal their courage and eloquence.

SIMONNOT-GODARD

The Most Beautiful Pocket Squares in the World

In the early 1990s the young Benjamin Simonnot, a student at business school, was in London and Madrid prospecting for new opportunities and clients for his family business, Simonnot-Godard, armed solely with a small briefcase given to him by his grandfather. Since the early 1980s, things had been rough for the business, which was owned by Benjamin's uncle François Simonnot and specialized in luxury home textiles and fabrics for women's haute couture. The company was faltering despite its two centuries of history. The economic situation was all the more difficult because of the massive invasion of inferior fabrics from the other side of the world. High-quality products made according to the standards of traditional craft seemed to have gone out of style.

Thus it was Benjamin who, barely out of business school, decided to save the family company, first working as an independent agent and finally buying the firm from his uncle in 1999. With his wife, Gersende, he opted for a radical strategy, choosing to channel all the firm's expertise and workforce into producing just one article, and one that amounted to only a fraction of the company's production: the handkerchief and its smaller version,

the pocket square. This small accessory had largely fallen into disuse since the 1960s, and there was little prospect of a comeback in menswear at a time when sportswear was all the rage.

The idea was not simply to sell just one thing, but to offer the best of its kind, using the house's expertise and historical experience in fabrics of all kinds. Not only would Benjamin and Gersende save the company by dint of hard work and strength of purpose, but also they were about to reveal its excellence to the world, by producing pocket squares of extraordinary beauty and sophistication. Simonnot-Godard's pocket squares are now distributed by such prestigious boutiques as Barneys and Bergdorf Goodman in New York, the discerning Armoury in Hong Kong and famous shops on Savile Row in London. Since the late 2000s Simonnot-Godard has been playing in the major league.

Back to the French Revolution

For any luxury business claiming some skill in craftsmanship, it has become an almost compulsory marketing strategy to use the glib rhetoric of long-established foundation stones. Lately, some have even inscribed the date of their creation in their visual identity, like a corporate trophy. The more distant

An Ascot tie in cotton and silk.

All Simonnot-Godard's products are woven; they are never printed.

the date underneath the logo, the more it is supposed to act as a guarantee of the quality of their products, of their connection to traditional craft (which, as we know, is often far from the truth). I have seen a slew of companies come up with spectacular foundation dates. Such claims would have been met with disdain by marketing specialists only a decade ago, when the rule was to obliterate the past and underscore modernity and state-of-the-art technology.

Why such a keen interest in old family stories that international corporations are ready to invest top dollar in? Why should your uncle Bob, whose career was anything but remarkable, be posthumously catapulted into the seat of company founder when he acted as mere intern when he was a lad? Why such competition over dates and family stories that are more or less true (and, for the most part, impossible to check)? Because tradition is a selling point, and has been for more than a decade.

This all accounts for the fact that, in the twenty-first century, consumers have undertaken a passionate quest for anything with a vintage feel and a 'traditional' image, whether because it is old or because the company that produces it is. Our modern society so obsessed with immediacy is also, paradoxically, in thrall to memory, history and the flavour of eternity that goes along with the products one buys. The ontological depth one looks for in luxury purchases gives rise to a compulsive attraction to authenticity.

Among the competitors in this crazy race for historical legacy and century-old stories, Simonnot-Godard stands out as a brilliant example of what sets apart the truly great companies that actually deal with the preservation of tradition from those who merely jump on the 'established in eighteen-something' bandwagon. In the world of luxury, where marketing mavens scrutinize every detail of the ideal brand image, Benjamin Simonnot stands out as a strikingly different character. The recovery of the company that bears his name was spectacular, and something of a model.

Benjamin is honest. So honest, in fact, that he explains candidly that his company may have been founded in 1787 but with another name, by a Monsieur Bougrain, a fabric merchant specializing in house linen whose partner, Auguste Godard – Benjamin's ancestor – took over the business only in 1830. Benjamin also

explains how this family story was certainly not the idyllic plain sailing that is the norm in the glossy leaflets of other luxury companies. Keeping the company alive was no picnic.

When he decided to take over the family business in 1999, Benjamin did not inherit the company; instead, he bought it with his own money in order to try and save a business for which he cared, having inherited his grandfather's passion for it. Apart from this vivid passion, the legacy was in a dire state: the weaving workshop was obsolete, the organization was disastrous, there was absolutely no economic strategy and the managing methods clearly belonged to another era. And yet the splendid Simonnot-Godard pocket square you sport now is an authentic cotton or linen cambric square made in 2014 or 2015 in the very same way it was made decades before in Cambrai, the capital of cambric and linens. That is all because Benjamin Simonnot has striven obsessively to respect the methods, craft, skill and historical secrets of the *maison* Simonnot-Godard.

Since the manufacturing base available to him when he started out was inadequate, and there was the possibility of achieving better quality elsewhere in France, Benjamin decided in 2002 to move the weaving operation to Lyon (with its strong tradition of *canuts*, workers who specialized in weaving). He entrusted the bleaching and mercerizing process to a workshop in the Vosges mountains, a region renowned for the purity of its water (it is the French equivalent of the Biella region in Italy, the cradle of all the great woollen mills, set up there in order to benefit from the very purest water).

I don't think there is any equivalent to this kind of production, where fabrics travel all over France to make sure that each step of the process is the best it can be. It's a sign of Simonnot-Godard's genuine desire to offer uncompromisingly authentic craftsmanship. I cannot think of a more apposite example than Simonnot-Godard of the connection between the legitimate claim to ancient foundation and the achievement of producing objects that satisfy the expectations of traditional craftsmanship.

The Most Beautiful Pocket Squares

Simonnot-Godard pocket squares embody the quintessence of this useless and yet essential

Some of Simonnot-Godard's fine handkerchiefs have complex woven patterns.

Overleaf

A traditional white handkerchief.

accessory, in which passionate interest has been taken by the sartorial community in recent years. That is no surprise, since the firm's exclusive focus on the pocket square has been allied with the sharpest and most radical approach, going far beyond the demands of any other manufacturer to ensure an unparalleled touch, sheen and sturdiness.

Producing a Simonnot-Godard pocket square is a complicated process amounting to four months of work between the selection of a pattern from the company archive and the last finishing touch. Patterns chosen from the archive are replicated as closely as possible, with the same weave and colour. This can take a very long time, since Simonnot-Godard – unusually in the market – never uses print but rather weaves the pattern into the fabric. This means that once a pattern is chosen, the exact original colour for *each* thread must be identified and that thread dyed accordingly.

Of course, this kind of work requires surgical precision. Each linen or cotton thread is dyed using a colourfast deep soak to obtain the richest shade. This method is fastidious and time-consuming, but the results are unmatched by modern printing techniques: while a printed handkerchief will lose its brightness after being washed a few times, a colourfast one as woven by Simonnot-Godard will be unchanged even after being washed several hundred times.

The weaving is carried out on several looms, two of which are specially equipped with a Jacquard harness so as to be able to replicate the patterns in the company's archive. Incidentally, the number of warp and weft threads per centimetre has remained the same for more than a century. That *is* fascinating.

Once the weaving is done, the rolls of fabric are sent to a chemical finisher in the Vosges region, where they are bleached and mercerized. Mercerizing, a chemical treatment invented by John Mercer in 1844, gives the fabric a crisp, lustrous appearance with a more luxurious feel. Only after this very important and technical stage is completed is the fabric sent to the Simonnot-Godard workshop in northern France, near Cambrai, to be hand-rolled.

Rollin', Rollin', Rollin'. . .

Purists are particularly fastidious about one detail that is found on all Simonnot-Godard handkerchiefs: the hem must be hand-rolled by specialists, the *roulotteuses*, seamstresses who once plied their trade at home.

There are many imperatives to this time-consuming technique, which lends the pocket square an irresistible charm: the whipped hem must have four stitches to the centimetre, as unobtrusive as possible; the thread must be the same type and colour as that used to weave the fabric; the roller must not stop in the middle of a hem, for any break will considerably alter the linear flow and thickness, which must be extremely steady; and the fabric must be rolled very tightly to give the handkerchief a firm feel.

Rollers used to be in charge of fabric cutting and boxing, too. Unfortunately, while hand-rolling is an integral part of Simonnot-Godard's high standards, it is a skill that is gradually disappearing. The company is currently working on creating a workshop dedicated to hand-rolling, in order to train new workers.

A Name for the Future

Starting out with the legacy of a frail company, Benjamin and Gersende Simonnot have accomplished something tremendous that ought to command admiration and respect. Their company is now flourishing internationally, and its production is acknowledged in all corners of the world for its sheer quality and uniqueness. Even in Italy, absolutely no one can rival the excellence and sophistication of Simonnot-Godard's pocket squares – an accessory whose renaissance is squarely in step with that of men's style as a whole.

Simonnot-Godard's future seems promising, and it would not be surprising if the firm decided to branch out and apply its remarkable expertise to other luxury textiles. It stands as an impressive example of entrepreneurial drive, having managed to preserve ancestral crafts, and showing that despite the rarity of skilled workers and the dreadful economic situation in Europe, it is still possible to succeed internationally with traditional products strictly made in France. *Ad augusta, per angusta.*

The pocket square is one gentlemen's requisite that has been coming back with some force since the beginning of the 2010s.

ADDRESS BOOK

Tailors

BERLUTI ATELIERS ARNYS
14 rue de Sèvres, 75007 Paris
www.berluti.com

CAMPS DE LUCA
16 rue de la Paix, 75002 Paris
www.campsdeluca.com

CIFONELLI BESPOKE
31 rue Marbeuf, 75008 Paris
www.cifonelli.com

SMALTO COUTURE
44 rue François Premier, 75008 Paris
www.smalto.com

Shoes

AUBERCY
34 rue Vivienne, 75002 Paris
www.aubercy.com

BERLUTI BESPOKE
26 rue Marbeuf, 75008 Paris
www.berluti.com

CORTHAY
1 rue Volney, 75002 Paris
www.corthay.com

DIMITRI GOMEZ
c/o Crockett & Jones
14 rue Chauveau-Lagarde, 75008 Paris
www.dimitribottier.com

JOHN LOBB BESPOKE
32 rue de Mogador, 75009 Paris
www.johnlobb.com

J. M. WESTON
243 rue Saint-Honoré, 75001 Paris
www.jmweston.fr

Shirts

CHARVET
28 place Vendôme, 75001 Paris

COURTOT
113 rue de Rennes, 75006 Paris
www.maison-courtot.com

HALARY
15 avenue Victor Hugo, 75116 Paris

LUCCA
58 boulevard des Batignolles,
75017 Paris

Trunks and Luggage

MOYNAT
348 rue Saint-Honoré, 75001 Paris
www.moynat.com

LOUIS VUITTON
101 avenue des Champs-Elysées,
75008 Paris
www.louisvuitton.com

Perfumery

CARON
90 rue du Faubourg Saint-Honoré,
75008 Paris
www.parfumscaron.com

GUERLAIN
68 avenue des Champs-Elysées,
75008 Paris
www.guerlain.com

Gentlemen's Requisites

CARTIER
13 rue de la Paix, 75002 Paris
www.cartier.fr

S. T. DUPONT
157 rue Saint-Honoré, 75001 Paris
www.st-dupont.com

MELLERIO DITS MELLER
9 rue de la Paix, 75002 Paris
www.mellerio.com

Bespoke Eyewear

BONNET
5 rue des Petits Champs, 75001 Paris
www.maisonbonnet.com

Men's Apparel

MARC GUYOT
5 & 8 rue Pasquier, 75008 Paris
www.marcguyot.com

Handkerchiefs

SIMONNOT-GODARD
See distributors' list on website
www.simonnot-godard.com

ACKNOWLEDGMENTS

For the past two years, as I was writing this book, I often caught myself wondering about the acknowledgments that would close the volume. Now that I have reached the end, I realize the impressive number of people who have been involved, sometimes briefly, sometimes at length, in turning out *The Parisian Gentleman*. I will now endeavour to thank them as I should.

First, my thanks go to the team of my online magazine, *Parisian Gentleman*, especially my luminous and beautiful partner in life, Sonya Glyn Nicholson, and my unwavering son, Greg Jacomet, for their constant support and the uniqueness of their personal talents. Creating *Parisian Gentleman* with my own family and working alongside people I love every day is a dream come true.

I also want to thank and congratulate Andy Julia for the astonishing quality of his pictures, which more than complement my writing as they practically speak for themselves. Andy is a great photographer and I hope this book will put him on the international map, as he truly deserves.

My gratitude also goes to:

- Jean Szlamowicz, who brilliantly translated this book into English with competence, patience, erudition and, above all, passion

- Samuel Clark, for his admirable artistic direction and for keeping a cool and clever head in the face of my doubts, uncertainties and constant delay

- Lucas Dietrich and Adélia Sabatini, my editors at Thames & Hudson, who trusted me all the way and with whom I am honoured to work

- My friends the photographers Lyle Roblin in Milan, Andy Barnham in London and Rose Callahan in New York for offering some of their beautiful pictures from their own work on Parisian style

- My two dear friends the very talented James Sherwood and G. Bruce Boyer, from London and New York, who wrote the forewords.

This book would not exist without the precious input of many essential players in Parisian elegance, especially:

- Adriano, Lorenzo and Massimo Cifonelli and Romain Le Dantec (Cifonelli)
- Marc and Julien de Luca (Camps de Luca)
- Julie Allanet (Smalto)
- Rémi Fritsch Fontanges and Marion Rochard (Berluti)
- Jean Grimbert
- Renaud Paul-Dauphin and Patrick Verdillon (John Lobb)
- Pierre Corthay and Xavier de Royère (Corthay)
- Philippe, Odette and Xavier Aubercy
- Julie Péresse and Cédric Dauch (J. M. Weston)
- Dimitri Gomez
- Paulus Bolten
- Patrice Halary
- Cydonia Courtot
- Jean-Claude Colban (Charvet)
- Valérie Viscardi and Julien Guerrier (Louis Vuitton)
- Guillaume Davin and Janie Zhuang (Moynat)
- Elisabeth Sirot and Thierry Wasser (Guerlain)
- Romain Alès, Chantal Evra and Richard Fraysse (Caron)
- Diane-Sophie Lanselle and Laurence de Vogue (Mellerio dits Meller)
- Michel Aliaga (Cartier)
- Valérie Chetrit and Anja Parfum (S. T. Dupont)
- Franck Bonnet, Steven Bonnet and Morgane Oudin-Maury (Bonnet)
- Marc Guyot
- Benjamin and Gersende Simonnot (Simonnot-Godard).

It should go without saying that I also thank all the readers of my online magazine *Parisian Gentleman* (www.parisiangentleman.fr and www.parisiangentleman.co.uk), wherever they are, for their loyalty and constant support.

This book is dedicated to the memory of Maxime Jacomet, my grandfather and the first bootmaker I've ever known, and to my mother, Janick Jacomet, the first seamstress in my life.

Hugo Jacomet

FURTHER READING

Nicholas Antongiavanni,
*The Suit: A Machiavellian Approach
   to Men's Style*
(New York, 2006)

Michèle Atlas and Alain Monniot,
Guerlain: Perfume Bottles since 1828
(Toulouse, 1997)

Honoré de Balzac,
Traité de la vie élégante
(Paris, 1922)

Jules Barbey d'Aurevilly,
Du Dandysme et de George Brummell
(Paris, 1997)

G. Bruce Boyer,
Gary Cooper: Enduring Style
(Brooklyn, NY, 2011)

Rose Callahan and Nathaniel Adams,
*I Am Dandy: The Return of the Elegant
   Gentleman*
(Berlin, 2013)

Alan Flusser,
*Dressing the Man: Mastering the Art
   of Permanent Fashion*
(New York, 2002)

Kate Irvin and Laurie Anne Brewer,
Artist, Rebel, Dandy: Men of Fashion
(New Haven, CT, 2013)

Hugo Jacomet,
*The Italian Gentleman: The Master Tailors
   of Italian Men's Fashion*
(London, 2017)

Dorothée Lagard,
*Francesco Smalto: 50 Ans d'élégance
   masculine*
(Paris, 2012)

Michèle Lécluse,
Moynat: La Réussite d'une audacieuse
(Suresnes, France, 2011)

Pierre Léonforté and Eric Pujalet-Plaà,
100 Legendary Trunks: Louis Vuitton
(New York, 2010)

Gilles Lipovetsky and Elyette Roux,
*Le Luxe Eternel: De L'âge du sacré au temps
   des marques*
(Paris, 2003)

Eric Musgrave,
Sharp Suits
(London, 2013)

Hans Nadelhoffer,
Cartier
(London, 2007)

Glenn O'Brien,
*How to Be a Man: A Guide to Style and Behavior
   for the Modern Gentleman*
(New York, 2011)

Paul-Gérard Pasols,
Louis Vuitton: The Birth of Modern Luxury
(New York, 2005)

James Sherwood,
Savile Row: The Master Tailors of British Bespoke
(London, 2010)
——,
*Fashion at Royal Ascot: Three Centuries of
   ThoroughbredStyle*
(London, 2011)
——,
*The Perfect Gentleman: The Pursuit of Timeless
   Elegance and Style in London*
(London, 2012)

Didier Van Cauwelaert,
J. M. Weston
(Paris, 2011)

PICTURE CREDITS

All photographs © Andy Julia unless otherwise indicated below.

Page 26
Top left: © Cifonelli.
Top right: © Smalto
Bottom: © Camps de Luca

Page 29
Photograph © Oleg Covian

Page 33
Top six photographs © Andy Barnham
    for Billionaire.com
Bottom two photographs © Rose
    Callahan

Pages 40–42, 49, 51
All images © Camps de Luca

Pages 57–58
Photograph © Smalto

Page 92
Top, left and right © Caulaincourt
Bottom, all images: © J. M. Weston

Page 93
Photograph © Altan Bottier

Page 115
Photograph © Berluti

Page 119
Photograph © Maison Corthay

Page 120
Photograph © Andy Barnham

Pages 120–25
All photographs © Maison Corthay

Page 128
Photograph © *The Rake* magazine

Page 129
Photograph © Maison Corthay

Pages 156, 159
All images © Maison Moynat

Page 165
Photograph © Collection Louis
    Vuitton/Antoine Jarrier

Page 166
Photograph © Collection Louis
    Vuitton/Antoine Jarrier

Page 168
Top, first three images from left:
    © Archives Louis Vuitton Malletier
Top right: © Archives Louis Vuitton
    Malletier/Dessin de Mich
Bottom: © Collection Louis Vuitton/
    Patrick Griès

Page 169
Photograph © Louis Vuitton Malletier/
    Patrick Griès

Page 172
Photograph © Louis Vuitton Malletier/
    Patrick Griès

Page 173
Bottom: © Collection Louis Vuitton/
    Antoine Jarrier

Pages 174, 176–78, 182
All photographs © Maison Moynat

Page 189
Photograph © Patrimoine Guerlain

Page 190
Photograph © Thibaut de
    Saint Chamas

Page 191
Photograph © Patrimoine Guerlain

Page 193
Top and middle: © Patrimoine
    Guerlain

Page 194
Top: © Patrimoine Guerlain

Page 196
Both photographs © Denis Chapoullié

Page 197
Below: © Denis Chapoullié

Page 240
Photograph © Lyle Roblin

Page 245
Photograph © Joël Saget

Pages 258–65
All photographs © Lyle Roblin

INDEX

Illustrations are indicated in *italic* and main page ranges are <u>underlined</u>